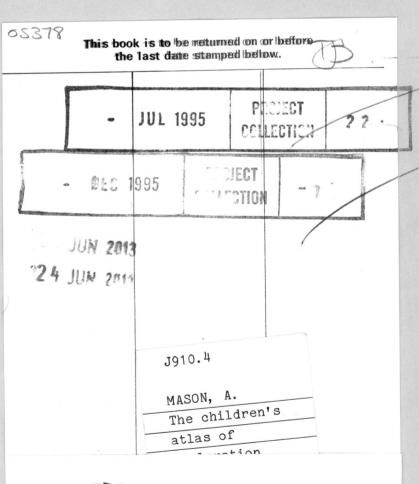

THE CHILDREN'S
ATLAS OF
EXPLORATION

THE CHILDREN'S
ATLAS OF
EXPLORATION

FOLLOW IN THE FOOTSTEPS OF
THE GREAT EXPLORERS

ANTONY MASON

THE
APPLE
PRESS

A QUARTO BOOK

Published by The Apple Press
6 Blundell Street
London N7 9BH

ISBN 1-85076-470-0

This book was designed and produced by
Quarto Publishing plc
The Old Brewery, 6 Blundell Street, London N7 9BH

Consultant Keith Lye
Creative Director Nick Buzzard
Senior Editor Cynthia O'Brien
Editor Michael Johnstone
Designer Martin Lovelock
Maps Janos Marffy
Illustrator Jim Robins
Picture Research Liz Eddison

The Publishers would like to thank the following for their help in the
preparation of this book: Malcolm Porter (Contour), Ben Goold,
Susan Millership, Karen Ball.

Typeset by Proteus Typesetters, Worle, England
Manufactured by Eray Scan Pte Ltd, Singapore
Printed by Star Standard Industries (Pte) Ltd, Singapore

CONTENTS

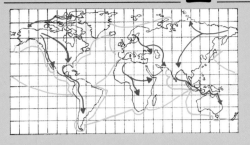

Exploration is as old as the human race. Natural curiosity has always driven people to discover what lies beyond the existing limits of their knowledge about the world. Exploration has taken many different forms and it is not always easy to say who is and who is not an explorer.

THE NEED TO EXPLORE

Curiosity is one of the great driving forces of human life. Over the last 100 000 years or so, the human race has been repeatedly asking the questions 'How?' and 'Why?'. Throughout the ages curiosity about the surrounding world has tempted people to explore — to find out what lies beyond the part of the world that they already know.

The nature of exploration has changed over time. Early human beings went out in search of better hunting grounds and safe places to live. The first farmers looked for fertile valleys where there was a reliable supply of water. Traders travelled to new lands to find new customers for their wares and to look for new goods to sell at home.

When the ancient civilizations of Mesopotamia, China, Egypt and Greece began to develop a respect for learning and knowledge, this led to a new kind of exploration: the search for knowledge for its own sake. Travellers would set out to find the answers to questions that intrigued them. What lay beyond those mountains? Where did this river begin? Where did that river reach the sea? There was only one way to find out, and that was to travel into the unknown, which has always needed courage and daring.

Below Many explorers went in search of new lands to settle. Some communities, such as this one of rice farmers in Borneo, have never settled, but use small areas of land until these are exhausted.

Right In the pursuit of knowledge about the world, geographers and mapmakers have to piece together all the information brought home by travellers, traders and explorers.

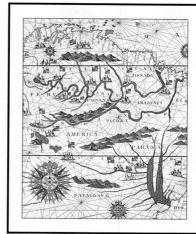

Mapping the world

From the 15th century on, European explorers realized the value of good maps. They took great care to make them accurate, as the coast of this 16th-century map of South America shows. By the 18th century, the desire to map the whole world was paramount.

Below Some early maps of the world are basically images which reflect a religion or philosophy. In this 13th-century French map, much of the northern hemisphere is occupied by Christian countries of the Mediterranean. Zodiac signs straddle the Equator.

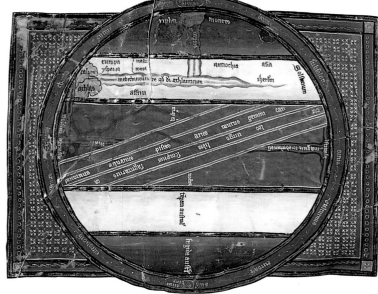

Above Rumours, myths and tall tales about monsters and strange occurrences in remote lands and oceans made the idea of distant travel seem doubly dangerous to early explorers. Illustrations such as this one, dated 1539, offered little comfort. Such pictures may have been based on genuine reports by travellers, but it is difficult to describe any animal from memory to someone who has never seen it.

Forgotten heroes

Until recent centuries, very little exploration was carried out for the sake of knowledge alone. Marco Polo (pictured here with his caravan of camels on a map made in 1375) set out on his 24-year voyage to China and the Far East in the hope of becoming rich by trade. He became famous mainly because he told of his adventures in a book, although only a few people read it at the time. But if it had not been for his chance meeting with a writer during a three-year spell as a prisoner of war in Genoa, this book might never have been written.

Numerous navigators, travellers and traders have been forgotten because they did not leave records of their voyages. For example, over 3 000 years ago the Polynesian navigators sailed vast distances across the Pacific Ocean in their flimsy outrigger boats in search of new lands, yet their achievements are now only vaguely remembered in myths. In many such cases, records were not needed at the time; in others, the records have been lost; and in the case of some, their discoveries were deliberately kept secret so that rival traders or nations would not profit from their efforts.

THE REAL EXPLORERS

The classic image of the true explorer is of a person travelling in great hardship through uncharted lands, patiently making maps and keeping records of everything observed — the land, people, animals and plants — while fighting off fearsome diseases, dangerous animals and hostile natives. But exploration can take many forms, and who really deserves to be given the title of explorer is often hard to say.

It is easier to recognize those who are clearly not explorers. Tourists, for example, may travel to remote places, but they are not explorers. Conquering generals are not usually thought to be explorers — yet sometimes they were accompanied by surveyors and mapmakers who did explore and find out more about the lands they invaded. Travelling to an unknown country and staying there is not exploration either. People who do this are thought of as settlers, not explorers, although some inquisitive settlers who ventured beyond these settlements to see what they could discover can be considered as explorers.

To take all such problems into account, the definition of an explorer has to remain rather vague. Thus, an explorer is someone who travels to places which are previously unknown to his or her people, gathers and records knowledge about these places, and then takes or sends this knowledge back home.

Discovery

It is often claimed that explorers *discover* new lands. For example, it used to be said that Christopher Columbus discovered the Americas when he sailed across the Atlantic to the Caribbean Islands in the *Santa Maria* (above) in 1492. The word 'discover', however, gives a misleading impression. These islands were already inhabited by Arawaks and Caribs.

Columbus found places about which he — and the rest of Europe — previously knew nothing. It was a discovery only from the European point of view. The fact that he went on to rename many of the islands, and to claim them for Spain, was typical of the behaviour of European explorers during the 15th and 16th centuries. Such arrogance and aggression has given the term 'discovery' a bad name.

Left Some of the early explorers were ruthless and greedy, particularly in the case of many of the Spanish in Central and South America.

Below Explorers travel to improve our knowledge of the world. Anthropologists study people such as these Ika Indians in Colombia.

Above European exploration changed in the 18th century when the thirst for trade and territory began to be replaced by the more gentle pursuits of geography and science. The French explorer La Pérouse, here seen on Easter Island, was an example of this new, less aggressive type of explorer.

Right *Skylab 1*, orbiting the Earth, points to the new dimension for exploration: space. Although it involves a level of technology quite unknown in previous eras, space travel has many aspects in common with the best time-honoured traditions of exploration.

The world is a jigsaw puzzle

Each community in the world builds up its own knowledge about the world. For example, a European's understanding of the world is quite different from that of a Tuareg nomad in the Sahara Desert. We cannot say that one is better than the other. The Tuaregs' knowledge of the Sahara is far more useful to them than the Europeans' idea of the world would be.

The world is like a jigsaw puzzle. Each piece is a different community that has its own view of the world, and its own knowledge about it. Likewise each community has its own explorers, who travel into other pieces of the jigsaw and bring back knowledge of them. The information that is gained helps them to see how neighbouring pieces fit in with their own. The ultimate goal has always been to complete the jigsaw.

SECTION 2 : EUROPE

Explorers, traders, settlers, conquerors and missionaries have all played their part in mapping Europe. Tribes and nations have jostled each other for territory and dominance, and in the 15th century this restless urge stimulated Europeans into venturing overseas.

EARLY CIVILIZATIONS

Human beings arrived in Europe some 100 000 years ago, probably from northern Africa, spreading north about 11 000 years ago.

The earliest European civilizations developed in the eastern Mediterranean from around 2000 BC with the Minoans (centring on the island of Crete) and the Mycenaeans (on mainland Greece). The city-states of Ancient Greece developed from around 1000 BC. By about 750 BC both the Greeks and the Phoenicians had explored much of the Mediterranean and created trading colonies.

The Ancient Greek civilization was the first in Europe to attempt to analyse the world in a scientific way. Geographers and astronomers used observation, and information from travellers, to make maps of the Mediterranean and the world.

Below The Greek-Egyptian astronomer Ptolemy worked in the Library of Alexandria from AD 127 to 150. He brought together all of Greek learning about geography to produce a world map. It remained the best world map until the 15th century. The original is lost.

Above The Phoenicians were master shipbuilders and the greatest traders of the Mediterranean. This relief carving made in 702 BC shows a Phoenician galley. By this time the Phoenicians had established colonies throughout the Mediterranean.

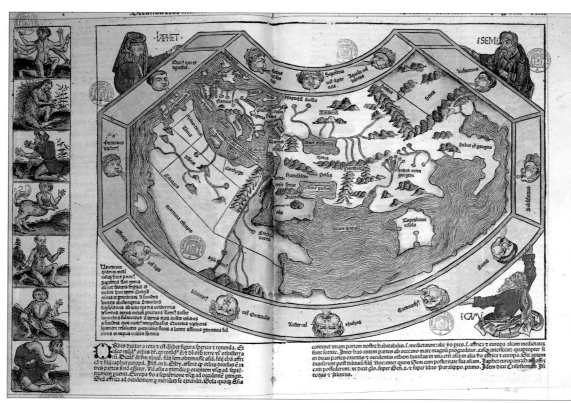

Above The Greek god Atlas is often portrayed carrying the world on his shoulders. Although there were many theories about the shape of the Earth, in around 200 BC the mathematician Eratosthenes calculated the circumference of the world, and miscalculated by just 250 km (155 miles).

The ends of the world

According to the Ancient Greeks, Hercules created the headlands at either side of the Strait of Gibraltar during his tenth labour when he had to obtain the oxen of the monster Geryon from Erythia.

For many years the Greeks regarded the Pillars of Hercules as the eastern extremity of their world. Beyond them lay the world's edge.

Between 310 and 306 BC, the Greek explorer Pytheas of Marseilles sailed through the Pillars, up the Atlantic coast of what is now Portugal and, it is said, circumnavigated Britain before sailing for home. Pytheas sailed not for trading reasons, but through real scientific interest.

Left Some people believe that Pytheas of Marseilles may have visited the Faroe Islands in the north Atlantic on his voyage of exploration that extended the Greeks' knowledge of the world beyond the Mediterranean.

Below Human development in Europe generally followed a northward direction after the first inhabitants spread out from Asia and Africa. Farming and town-dwelling civilizations spread north from their early centres in the eastern Mediterranean.

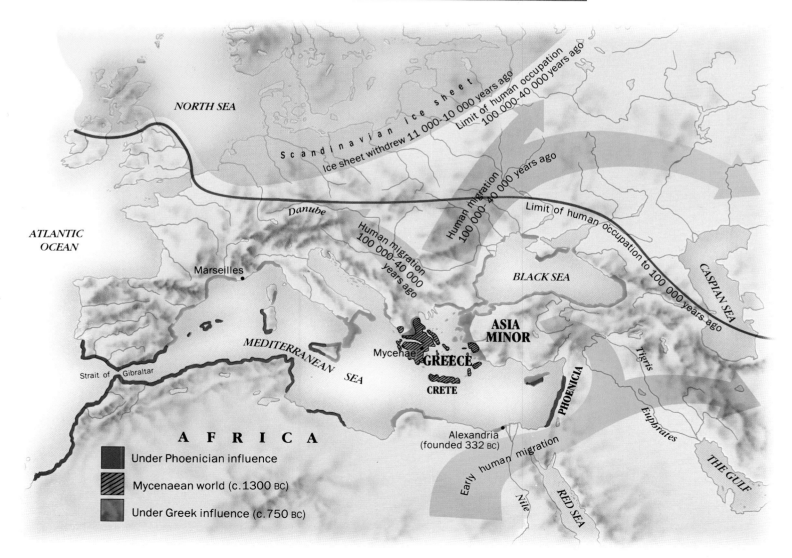

Under Phoenician influence

Mycenaean world (c.1300 BC)

Under Greek influence (c.750 BC)

THE ROMAN WORLD

The Romans continued to expand on the knowledge of the world which the Greeks had established. But their intentions were rather different. The work of the Roman mapmakers and surveyors was essentially about creating and maintaining an empire.

At its largest, the Roman Empire included all the lands bordering the Mediterranean, and east as far as Mesopotamia (modern Iraq), and all of western Europe as far north as Britain where Hadrian's Wall marked the northernmost extent of their conquests.

The Romans also knew about India from the campaigns of Alexander the Great (see pages 24–25), and they had some idea about the Far East because trade goods from China reached the Roman world by way of the Silk Road (see pages 22–23). None the less they rarely ventured beyond their own boundaries.

The Romans did, however, travel extensively within the Empire. Both the Ancient Greeks and Romans produced books and travel guides for sightseers. A famous example of this is *Hellados Periegesis* ('Guided Tour of Greece'), written in the 2nd century AD by the Greek author Pausanias.

Above The Romans conquered what they called 'Africa' (modern Tunisia) in the 2nd century BC, and built Dougga on the site of an old Phoenician city. As a way of expressing their power over conquered lands, the Romans liked to build monuments on a grand scale, even in the most remote corners of their Empire.

Right The Roman Empire reached its largest extent in the 2nd century AD, when the Romans controlled the entire Mediterranean, as well as all neighbouring countries — which they occupied in order to protect the Mediterranean. The conquest of Britain was an exception to this general strategy.

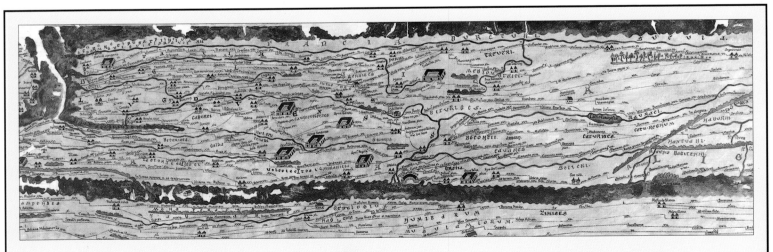

All roads lead to Rome

The Romans were great road-builders, because they knew that they had to have good communications in order to rule their Empire effectively. The shortest distance between two points is a straight line, so they built their roads as straight as possible to make the quickest routes for sending supplies and messengers — and armies in case of trouble. Even today in many parts of Europe, modern roads follow the same routes taken by the old Roman roads. You can often recognize such roads because they are so straight and because they continue for such extraordinarily long distances.

Maps were made of these roads for the use of the administrators and generals. The 'Table of Peutinger' (above) is a 6.8 m (22.3 ft) long map which shows the Roman Empire in a simplified form. It marks roads and the distances between towns.

The 'Table of Peutinger' is probably a 13th-century copy of an original made in the 3rd or 4th century AD. It was discovered in Germany in the 15th century and is named after Konrad Peutinger, who owned it after 1507.

Right Hadrian's Wall marked the most northerly limit of the Roman Empire (below). The wall stretched some 120 km (74 miles) across northern England, almost from coast to coast, and was built under orders from Emperor Hadrian in the 120s and 130s AD.

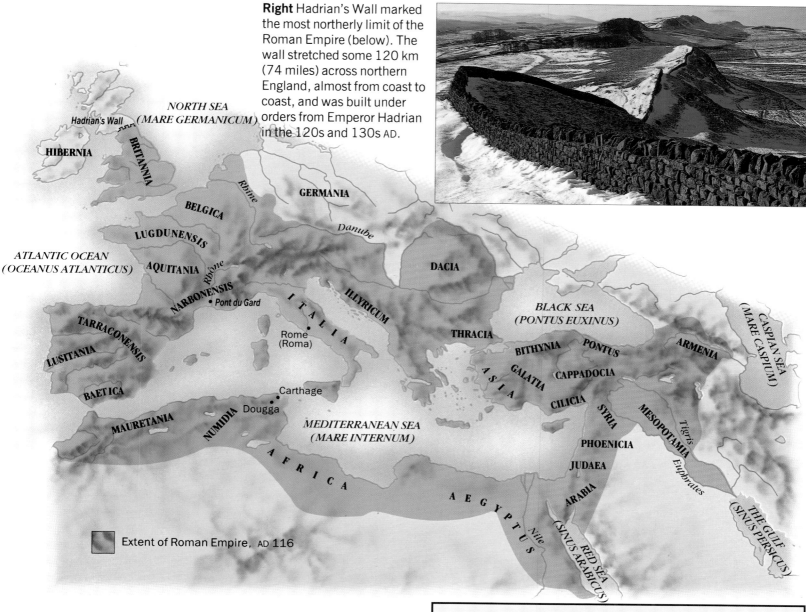

HIBERNIA

BRITANNIA

Hadrian's Wall

NORTH SEA
(MARE GERMANICUM)

Rhine

GERMANIA

Danube

BELGICA

LUGDUNENSIS

ATLANTIC OCEAN
(OCEANUS ATLANTICUS)

AQUITANIA

Rhône

DACIA

NARBONENSIS

• Pont du Gard

ILLYRICUM

I T A L I A

TARRACONENSIS

Rome
(Roma)

THRACIA

BLACK SEA
(PONTUS EUXINUS)

LUSITANIA

BITHYNIA

PONTUS

ARMENIA

CASPIAN SEA
(MARE CASPIUM)

A S I A

GALATIA

CAPPADOCIA

BAETICA

Carthage

CILICIA

SYRIA

MESOPOTAMIA

MAURETANIA

NUMIDIA

Dougga

MEDITERRANEAN SEA
(MARE INTERNUM)

PHOENICIA

Tigris

Euphrates

A F R I C A

JUDAEA

THE GULF
(SINUS PERSICUS)

A E G Y P T U S

ARABIA

Nile

RED SEA
(SINUS ARABICUS)

■ Extent of Roman Empire, AD 116

Below The Pont du Gard in the south of France was built as an aqueduct in the 1st century BC. It shows engineering skills that remained unmatched for hundreds of years after the Roman Empire collapsed.

Masters of the seas

Until the 3rd century BC the Phoenicians possessed the finest fleet in the Mediterranean. The Romans learnt the secrets of Phoenician ship design by studying a wreck. They took control of the sea, and of trade throughout the Mediterranean, in 260 BC during the first war against the powerful Phoenician colony of Carthage. This wall-painting shows grain being loaded onto a merchant ship at Ostia, the port of Rome. Goods could be moved quite quickly as a Roman cargo ship such as this could travel about 160 km (100 miles) a day. The men who rowed were galley slaves, often the citizens of conquered lands who were dragooned into the galleys.

BARBARIANS AND MISSIONARIES

The Roman Empire was already in decline by the 5th century AD when a series of attacks by fearsome armies from eastern Europe brought it to its knees. By AD 476 the old Roman Empire had collapsed. However, the first Christian emperor of Rome, Constantine I, who ruled from AD 306 to 337, had founded Constantinople (now Istanbul in modern Turkey), and this became the centre of the Christian Byzantine Empire which lasted until the 15th century.

Much of the learning of the ancient, classical world was lost in this turbulent period, and even more was lost over the following centuries. The Christian Church remained the main source of learning in Europe for at least the next 1 000 years.

Some of the great travellers of these centuries were Christian missionaries, who set out to spread the Gospel to the pagan tribes that occupied much of the old Roman Empire. Although it had never become a Roman territory, Ireland was converted to Christianity after about AD 440. A number of missionaries travelled out from there to take Christianity to the peoples of continental Europe. St Brendan may even have reached America.

Above Many early Christians lived as hermits, shutting themselves away from the world and devoting their lives to prayer and contemplation. These very simple stone huts, known as *clochans* or beehive cells, were built by Irish Christians in about AD 800.

Below The Visigoths, led by King Alaric I, destroyed Rome in AD 410, as shown in this painting. They later conquered Roman provinces in Spain and Gaul. The Vandals took Roman North Africa in AD 429. Italy was attacked by the Huns in AD 452.

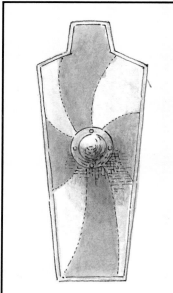

The original Vandals

The collapse of the Roman Empire can be traced back to about AD 370 when the Huns of central Asia began attacking the Germanic tribes of eastern Europe, such as the Vandals and Goths, who in turn attacked the Romans to the west. These peoples were known to the Romans as 'barbarians', which meant 'uncivilized and foreign'. In AD 476, Odovacar led his vast Barbarian army into Italy, took over and declared himself king. Barbarians now controlled the western Roman Empire.

Left A granite high cross at Castledermot, County Kildare, dating from the 9th century AD, shows the distinctive intertwining patterns of Irish Celtic art. This can also be seen on their jewellery and church treasures. Despite repeated attacks by the Vikings (see pages 16–17), for about 400 years the monasteries of Ireland provided one of the great centres for learning, art and culture in Europe.

Below The Huns, Goths and Vandals had taken over most of the Roman world by the end of the 5th century AD. In the following centuries Christianity spread out from its main centres in Rome and Constantinople (now Istanbul), as well as from Ireland.

Was it America?

St Brendan (about AD 484–577) was one of the major figures of the early Irish Church and founded a number of important monasteries. He was also a great traveller, and is the hero of a saga called *Navigatio Sancti Brendani* which was translated into several European languages. This describes his seven-year sea-voyage, accompanied by 12 disciples, in which he discovers the 'Land Promised to Saints'. It is widely believed that the story is based on a true voyage, and that St Brendan may even have reached America.

→ Expansion of Christianity, 6th — 9th centuries
→ Monastic expansion from Ireland
Areas under control of Germanic invaders in AD 493

■ Ostrogoths
■ Burgundians
■ Franks
■ Visigoths
■ Vandals

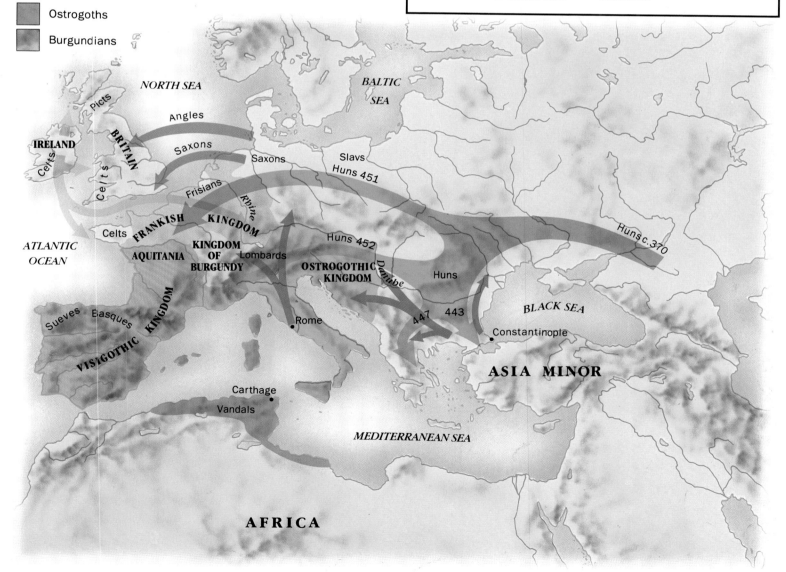

VIKING TRAVELLERS

For three centuries after AD 800 the sight of a Viking warship would bring terror to the towns and villages that lined the coasts of western Europe. The Vikings were ruthless raiders. They came to steal food, cattle and treasure from the churches and monasteries, and to capture strong and healthy young men and women to sell as slaves.

The Vikings came from the lands now known as Norway, Sweden and Denmark. Although they are remembered mainly as raiders, they were also settlers and traders. By the 11th century there were Viking settlements across northern Europe from Russia to Ireland. Trading expeditions took them as far as the Mediterranean Sea and down the River Volga to the Caspian Sea.

They settled in Iceland from around AD 870. In about AD 986 Erik the Red, an adventurer who had been banished from Norway for murder, sailed on from Iceland to found the Eastern Settlement, a colony in Greenland around Brattahlid.

Fourteen years later, Erik the Red's son, Leif Eriksson, set off on a voyage of exploration and found three new lands which he named Helluland, Markland and Vinland.

The true location of Vinland could only be guessed at until the 1960s when the remains of a Viking settlement were found on the coast of Newfoundland, showing that the Vikings were probably the first Europeans to reach the Americas.

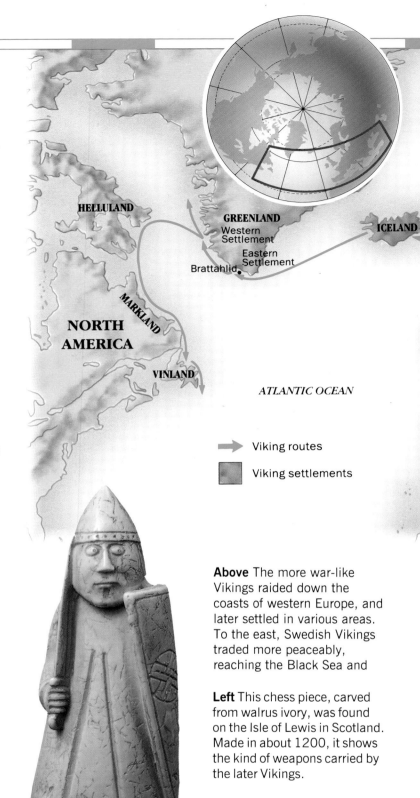

Above The more war-like Vikings raided down the coasts of western Europe, and later settled in various areas. To the east, Swedish Vikings traded more peaceably, reaching the Black Sea and

Left This chess piece, carved from walrus ivory, was found on the Isle of Lewis in Scotland. Made in about 1200, it shows the kind of weapons carried by the later Vikings.

Left This memorial stone from Gotland, Sweden shows the delicate quality of Viking craftsmanship. The lower part illustrates a Viking warship. The upper part shows a warrior approaching Valhalla, where Viking heros were said to go after death in battle.

Right In Iceland the Vikings found a landscape similar to the rocky fjords of their homelands. The search for new and better farming land to feed an increasing population may have been one reason why the Vikings began raiding.

FAROE
ISLANDS

SHETLAND
ISLANDS

NORTH
SEA Danes

BRITAIN
AND

Norwegians

SCANDINAVIA

Swedes

BALTIC SEA

• Novgorod

K I E V A N

• Kiev

Volga

R U S S I A

CASPIAN SEA

CALIPHATE
OF
CORDOBA

ITALY

Constantinople *BLACK SEA*

BYZANTINE EMPIRE

MEDITERRANEAN SEA

NORTH AFRICA

the Caspian Sea, where they came into contact with the Arab world. Western expeditions to Iceland, Greenland and North America were carried out by settlers in search of land.

Right The monks in Ireland built massive 'round towers' in which to hide from Viking raiders. The stone walls were about 2 m (6.6 ft) thick at the base. The monks used a ladder to reach the entrance, which was set at least 4 m (13 ft) off the ground.

Longships and knorrs

From the 8th to the 11th century AD, the Vikings were the most skilled boatbuilders and seamen in northern Europe. Their raiding parties used longships of up to 28 m (92 ft) in length, driven by a single rectangular sail and 16 pairs of oars.

Longships were built of overlapping planks of wood and were double-ended: the stern looked the same as the bow. They were steered by an oar called a *steerboard* fixed to one side (hence our term starboard).

Cargo ships, called *knorrs*, were constructed in a similar way but tended to be much wider. The Vikings may have made their journeys across the Atlantic in *knorrs*.

Viking treasure

Collections of Viking treasures have been discovered all over Europe. Not all of these had been stolen. The Vikings were gifted craftsmen and made beautiful jewellery for themselves, while the large hoards of silver coins could well have been the profits from successful trading ventures. The presence of Arab coins in a treasure hoard found in Sweden (right) demonstrates that their trading links extended at least as far as the Middle East.

THE RENAISSANCE AND EUROPEAN EXPANSION

Towards the end of the medieval period from the 5th to the 15th century, there was a gradual change of mood in Europe which has become known as the Renaissance, or 'rebirth'. It was inspired by a new appreciation of the achievements of the Ancient Greeks and Romans. The Renaissance brought fresh ideas to all areas of learning.

'Renaissance men' represented the spirit of the age. They enjoyed using any talent they might possess and led energetic lives as artists, poets, scholars, politicians, soldiers and adventurers, often sponsored by enlightened European monarchs.

When such people looked at the maps of the time, they saw just how much remained to be discovered. Very little was known about Africa or Asia, except that these were the sources of gold, spices, silk and precious stones. Previously these goods had been traded across the Mediterranean by middlemen, such as the Arabs, but few Europeans knew what lay beyond the Mediterranean ports.

In the 15th century European traders and adventurers set out to discover the way to the East. By the end of the century they had reached India and the Americas; by 1522 they had travelled right around the world.

Above Because medieval mapmakers often invented geography so as to present an image of the world that reflected Christian teaching (for example, they might start by placing Jerusalem at the centre), navigators in the 15th century used maps first made by the Greeks and Romans.

Below The Belem Tower, built in 1515, stands beside the River Tagus in Lisbon, Portugal. Many explorers passed beneath its walls on their way to new worlds in Africa, the Far East and South America. Within a few years similar fortresses had been built around the world.

The tools of exploration

A variety of navigational instruments came into general use during the 15th century, such as the compass, dividers, hourglass, star charts and tables which all became part of the navigator's kit. The backstaff was used to measure the angle of the sun, from which a ship's latitude could be calculated. With such instruments navigators could work out their precise position and chart their voyages accurately.

Below Although many peoples sent out expeditions to explore the world, it was the Europeans who were the first to attempt to explore the world systematically. Spreading out from their home ports, they reached most of the coastal regions of the world in less than a century.

A ship for explorers

The Portuguese *caravel* was well suited to exploration. At only 21 m (69 ft) in length, it was small by modern standards, and could be sailed by a crew of 20. It had a distinctive shape with a high 'poop' deck at the stern for the helmsman and navigator, and an equally high deck at the bow. However, the breadth of the ship (7.5 m [24.6 ft]) and the rounded shape of the hull made it stable in heavy seas. As well as ordinary square sails, it also had triangular sails, a combination which greatly improved manoeuvrability in most winds.

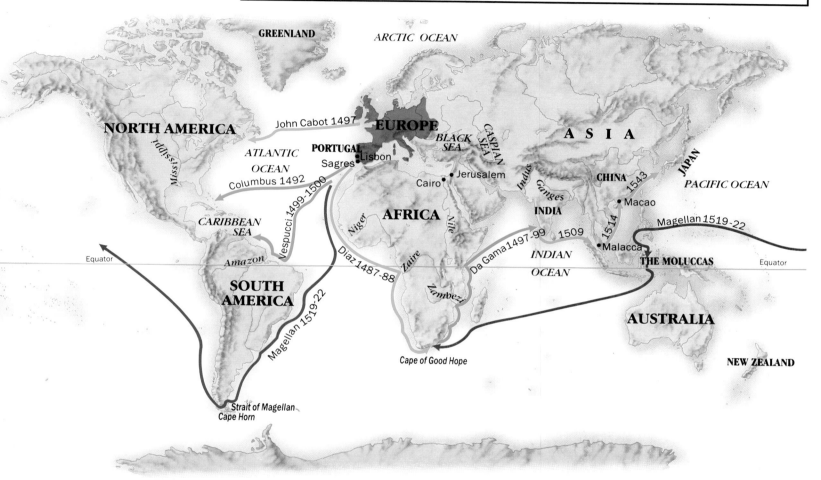

GREENLAND   ARCTIC OCEAN

NORTH AMERICA   John Cabot 1497   EUROPE   BLACK SEA   CASPIAN SEA   A S I A

Mississippi   ATLANTIC OCEAN   PORTUGAL   Lisbon   CHINA   1543   JAPAN   PACIFIC OCEAN

Sagres   Jerusalem   Columbus 1492   Cairo

CARIBBEAN SEA   *Niger*   AFRICA   *Nile*   INDIA   Macao   Magellan 1519-22

Vespucci 1499-1500   *Ganges*   *Indus*   1514   1509

Equator   *Amazon*   Diaz 1487-88   *Zaire*   Da Gama 1497-99   Malacca   THE MOLUCCAS   Equator

SOUTH AMERICA   INDIAN OCEAN

Magellan 1519-22   *Zambezi*   AUSTRALIA

Cape of Good Hope   NEW ZEALAND

Strait of Magellan
Cape Horn

Prince of navigators

The Portuguese were the first European seafarers to undertake exploration in a serious way. They owed much of their inspiration to Prince Henry (1394–1460), the son of King John I of Portugal and his English queen, Philippa. He set up a famous school of navigation at Sagres, which brought together the skills of navigators, geographers, mapmakers, astronomers and boatbuilders. He also helped to organize a number of early Portuguese expeditions. By the time of his death they had only reached the southern coasts of West Africa, but these were important first steps in the search for the route to the East.

He became known as 'Prince Henry the Navigator', although in fact he did not take part in any expeditions himself. Following his example, other schools of navigation were set up elsewhere in Europe, as depicted in this imaginative 1670 engraving, despite the fact that the voyages he financed left him in debt when he died.

SECTION 3: ASIA

For thousands of years merchants and adventurers travelled along the trade routes that spanned Asia. But its mountains and areas of wilderness and desert ensured that its more remote corners remained unexplored until the 20th century.

FIRST CITIES

The origin of the word 'civilization' is closely linked to the idea of citizens and cities. Towns and cities can only exist where people are well organized: they depend on farms to support them, on systems of trade, and on all kinds of professions to make them function properly. They also need efficient systems of law and government, and usually have well-developed religions.

Many of the world's first cities grew up in Asia, around 5 000 years ago. This followed on from the development of farming in about 9000 BC. Communities of farmers settled in the fertile lands around the major rivers, such as the Tigris and Euphrates in Mesopotamia, the Indus in southern Asia, and the Yellow River, Huang He, in China. As their farming became more efficient, their villages developed into towns, then cities. The first people to settle in Mesopotamia were the Sumerians who, after about 3500 BC, established centres of

civilization which became known as city-states. These encouraged the development of national identity among the people.

The civilizations of Mesopotamia, the Indus Valley and China all developed along similar lines. They used the wheel for transport; they developed networks of trade with many neighbouring regions; each had its own form of writing. There was some communication between Mesopotamia and the civilizations of southern Asia. China, however, is walled in by the massive ridge of mountains that curls round the huge deserts of central Asia. It grew up more or less in isolation until trade routes opened up across the continent in the 2nd century BC.

The vast continent of Asia contains dramatic extremes of landscape and climate, including the Himalayas and Karakoram mountains, the burning deserts of Arabia and the huge steppes of northern Asia, which lie frozen for much of the year. These have provided many of the greatest challenges in exploration.

Left Babylon was one of the world's first great cities and grew to become the capital of one of the major empires of Mesopotamia.

Below This clay tablet includes a very early map of the world with Babylon at the centre.

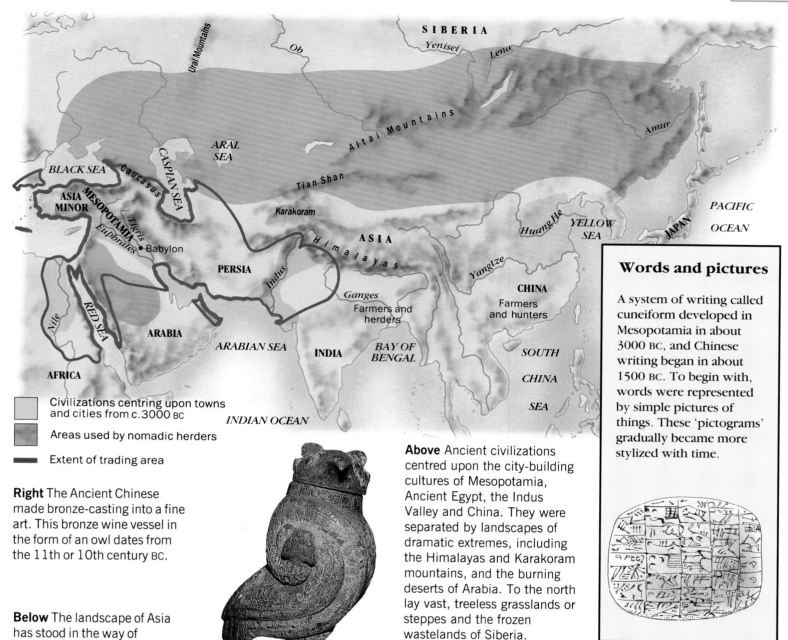

Civilizations centring upon towns and cities from c.3000 BC

Areas used by nomadic herders

Extent of trading area

Right The Ancient Chinese made bronze-casting into a fine art. This bronze wine vessel in the form of an owl dates from the 11th or 10th century BC.

Below The landscape of Asia has stood in the way of travellers, but has also provided protection from intruders. This fort is in the Hunza region of Pakistan.

Above Ancient civilizations centred upon the city-building cultures of Mesopotamia, Ancient Egypt, the Indus Valley and China. They were separated by landscapes of dramatic extremes, including the Himalayas and Karakoram mountains, and the burning deserts of Arabia. To the north lay vast, treeless grasslands or steppes and the frozen wastelands of Siberia.

Words and pictures

A system of writing called cuneiform developed in Mesopotamia in about 3000 BC, and Chinese writing began in about 1500 BC. To begin with, words were represented by simple pictures of things. These 'pictograms' gradually became more stylized with time.

Birthplace of religions

Hinduism, Buddhism, Judaism, Christianity and Islam all began in Asia, and are all closely connected to the development of civilization. Hinduism dates back 4 000 years and gave rise to some of the earliest great works of literature. The *Ramayana* tells the story (above) of how Prince Rama engages the help of the monkey army to rescue his wife, Sita. Hinduism is still the established faith in India, where it is practised by millions of followers.

EARLY CHINESE EXPLORERS

Chinese civilization began in around 1700 BC, yet it took China over 1 000 years to make regular contact with the civilizations of western and southern Asia. In 138 BC Chang Ch'ien (died about 112 BC) was sent to central Asia by Emperor Wu Ti (reigned 140–86 BC) to try to arrange treaties with peoples on the Chinese western borders against the invading Huns. He was away for 12 years, 10 of which he spent as a captive of the Huns. After he escaped, he tried to return to China via Tibet but was recaptured, although he eventually returned home. His mission was a failure, but he brought back news of trading opportunities with western Asia. As a result, new trade routes soon opened up, carrying such goods as spices, gems and silk across the Gobi Desert and the high mountains of central Asia to the Middle East and Europe. There were several routes which became known generally as the 'Silk Road'.

Many of the early Chinese travellers to central and southern Asia were Buddhists in search of religious knowledge in and around northern India, the homeland of Buddhism. The most famous was Hsüan Tsang (AD 596–664). He travelled for 16 years across central Asia to Kashmir and India, and along the River Ganges and was welcomed home by the Emperor. This was unusual, however, for travel beyond China's borders was not encouraged, and foreigners were kept out. For this reason the advanced state of China's civilization remained virtually unknown to the West until Marco Polo's travels in the 13th century.

Below The Silk Road carried not only trade but also ideas. At Bezeklik, near Turfan, ancient Buddhist caves line the thin ribbon of fertile land beside the river.

Right The Great Wall of China was begun in the 5th century BC and was more or less complete by 221 BC, although it was rebuilt and extended over a period of 2 000 years. Stretching for 3 460 km (2 150 miles), it was built to keep warring northern tribes out of China. For most Chinese it also marked the limit of civilization: beyond lay an unknown and barbaric world which they did not care to visit.

The costliest cloth

Silk is manufactured by spinning the fibres from the cocoons of silkworms (right), the caterpillars of a moth which feed on mulberry trees. According to legend, silk has been made since 2640 BC. The embroidered phoenix (left), found in the Altai mountains of central Asia, dates from the 4th century BC and is thought to be the oldest piece of silk in existence.

Silk cloth is very fine and has always been expensive. For thousands of years it was made only in China. In the 6th century AD, however, some silkworm eggs were smuggled out of China and taken to Constantinople (Istanbul). From these smuggled eggs, the development of the European medieval silk industry began.

Left War, trading opportunities and Buddhism were the main inspiration behind the journeys of the great early Chinese travellers, journeys which took them into inland Asia and well beyond the self-imposed limits of Chinese civilization.

Below This bronze relief statue of Hsüan Tsang is from a temple dedicated to him in Taiwan. Hsüan Tsang returned in triumph from his 16 years of travel with a caravan bearing priceless religious texts and sacred relics.

➡ Hsüan Tsang (AD 629-45)

➡ Chang Ch'ien (138-126 BC)

➡ Northern silk route

➡ Southern silk route

Left This gilt-bronze statue of a Bodhisattva (Buddha-to-be) was made in China in the 10th century AD, about 1 000 years after Buddhism had spread into China from India.

ALEXANDER THE GREAT

Alexander (356–323 BC) was from Macedonia, a kingdom which came to dominate Greece during the reign of his father, King Philip II. As a boy, he was taught by the great philosopher Aristotle (384–322 BC).

When Alexander was 20 his father was murdered. He succeeded to the throne and began a series of conquests. In 334 BC he invaded the Persian Empire of Darius III (ruled 336–330 BC); in 332 BC he entered Egypt and was crowned pharaoh; in 331 BC he finally defeated Darius and won control of the Persian Empire.

All along he took great trouble to collect information about the geography of the regions which fell to his conquests. For example, he sent an expedition led by Heracleides to establish whether or not the Caspian Sea was attached to the Black Sea, a fact which several scholars believed to be the case.

After his victory over the Persians he led his army on a great voyage of conquest and exploration, reaching the remote regions of Parthia, Bactria and the Hindu Kush. By 326 BC he had reached the River Indus. By this time his armies were close to mutiny, so he turned back, taking the opportunity to send another expedition, under a general called Nearchus, to explore the Gulf by sea.

All this was achieved in 13 years. During this time Alexander had travelled 32 000 kilometres (20 000 miles) and founded 70 cities. Alexander was one of the greatest generals in history; yet when he died of fever in Babylon, he was just 32 years old.

Above Persepolis was destroyed by Alexander in 330 BC. It had been built as the grand ceremonial capital of the Persian Empire by King Darius I (ruled 522–486 BC), and only functioned fully once a year when ambassadors from all parts of the Empire came to deliver tribute to the king. The city was put to the torch by Alexander as an act of revenge for the earlier Persian burning of Athens.

Measured by strides

Alexander's armies were accompanied by teams of surveyors, geographers, mathematicians and astronomers. Some of these went ahead to plan the advance of the armies, others mapped the conquered territories which extended from the River Indus to the eastern Mediterranean. The surveyors included men called *bematistae*, who measured distances by counting their strides. They wore sandals such as those pictured above. European maps made over 1 500 years later still used information about Asia acquired during Alexander's conquests.

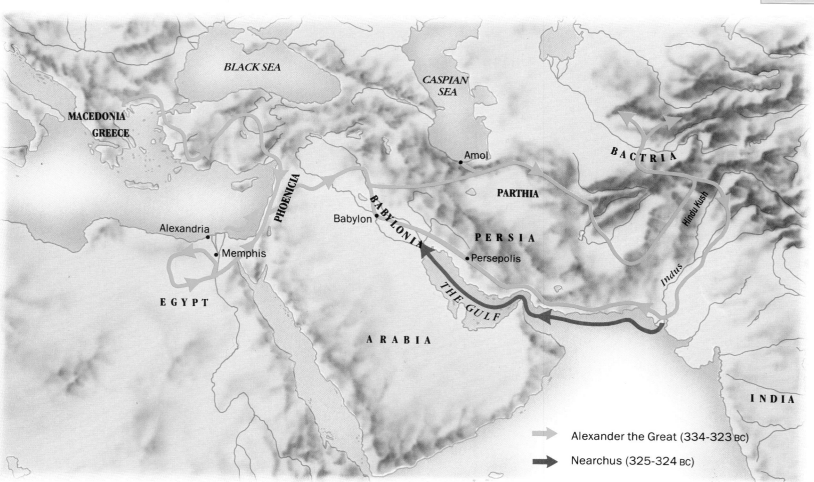

BLACK SEA

CASPIAN SEA

MACEDONIA
GREECE

Amol

BACTRIA

PARTHIA

Hindu Kush

PHOENICIA

Babylon

BABYLONIA

PERSIA

Alexandria

Persepolis

Indus

Memphis

THE GULF

EGYPT

ARABIA

INDIA

→ Alexander the Great (334-323 BC)

→ Nearchus (325-324 BC)

Above Alexander the Great swept through the eastern Mediterranean, destroying the Persian Empire. The thirst for exploration led him further east, where he collected information that was still being used 1 500 years later.

Below No other European conqueror has succeeded as Alexander did in waging campaigns across the high mountains and deserts of central Asia. But this landscape proved a tough and deadly challenge.

The library of Alexandria

Alexandria, on the coast of northern Egypt, was founded by Alexander in 332 BC. About 30 years after his death a library was built there which was to become one of the great centres of learning of the ancient world. By the 2nd century BC it contained some 700 000 books (mainly in the form of papyrus scrolls). It was also famous for its cartography. Eratosthenes (the Greek who calculated the circumference of the Earth) was a librarian there and Ptolemy was based at the library from AD 127–150 (see pages 10–11). It appears to have fallen from use by about the 7th century.

THE RISE OF ISLAM

From Roman times on, the Middle East was a vital link between East and West. Trade came from China along the Silk Road (see pages 22–23) and across the Middle East to ports on the Mediterranean coast, or by sea from South-East Asia and India to the Red Sea. Cities which controlled the trade routes soon became wealthy and powerful.

Muhammad (about AD 570–632), the prophet and founder of Islam, was born in Mecca, a trading city and an important religious centre. His new religion spread with remarkable speed, through conversion and conquest. Within a century of Muhammad's death, the Islamic Empire stretched from Spain in the west to Afghanistan in the east.

Islam quickly acquired a tradition for learning, and Muslim travellers set out across the Empire and beyond in a spirit of enquiry. Al-Masudi (died AD 956) was one of the great Islamic travellers, and author of some 30 books. He visited Sri Lanka, China and as far as the east coast of Africa.

The Islamic world also produced notable mapmakers and geographers, such as the north African Al-Idrisi (died about 1165). He travelled all over the Islamic Empire before producing his famous map of the world, which was based largely on Greek sources.

Above Muslims from northern Africa, known as the Moors, invaded Spain in AD 711, and parts of Spain remained under Muslim control until 1492. They built splendid mosques, and palaces such as this, the Alhambra in Granada.

Right The spread of Islam was swift and — with the sole major exception of Moorish Spain — lasting. By the 9th century it had taken over the entire southern Mediterranean and reached the borders of India.

Below The Kaaba, a cube-shaped stone building in the Great Mosque of Mecca, is the most sacred shrine of Islam. It contains the Black Stone which, according to tradition, is part of the first mosque, built by Abraham.

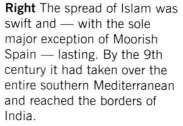

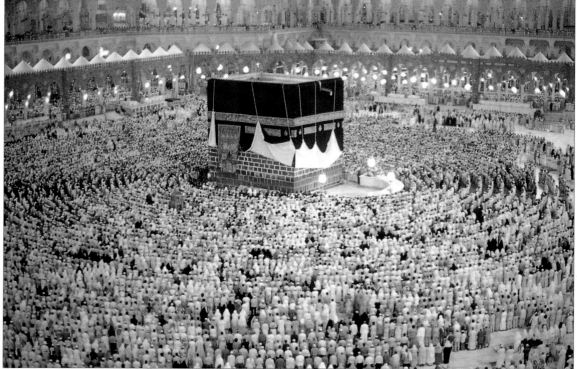

Guided by the stars

The Arabs developed a number of important navigational instruments. They learnt how to use the magnetic compass from the Chinese. They also perfected the astrolabe (above), a complex instrument for making calculations based on the stars which made them extremely skilled navigators.

Guardians of learning

Despite their reputation for conquest, the rulers of the new Islamic Empire had great respect for learning. Baghdad, the capital of the Empire after AD 762, became a centre for scholarship. While Europe descended into chaos, Islamic scholars led the world in medicine, astronomy and mathematics, taking advantage of their connections with India, China and the Greek scholars of Alexandria. They translated into Arabic the great works of Greek learning. These, as well as books by Arab writers, were later translated into Latin by European scholars during the Renaissance (see pages 18–19). This Latin translation (right) of an Arabic book, dating from the 13th century, shows a constellation represented in the form of an Arab-style ship.

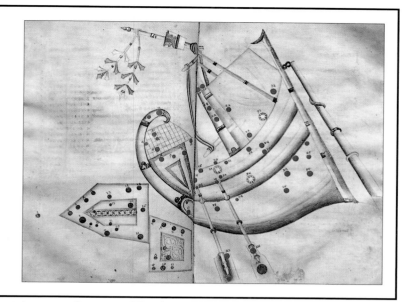

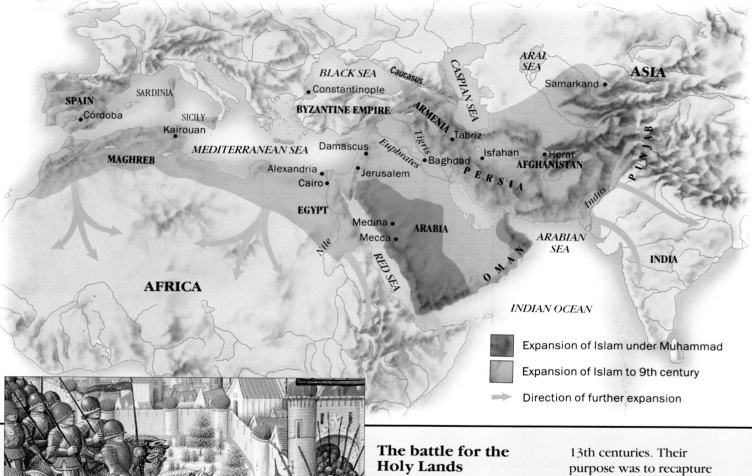

- Expansion of Islam under Muhammad
- Expansion of Islam to 9th century
- → Direction of further expansion

The battle for the Holy Lands

With the rise of Islam, the Christian world shrank. In earlier centuries the Christians had five main centres, or patriarchates. Jerusalem, Alexandria and Antioch were lost to Islam in the 7th century, leaving just Constantinople in modern-day Turkey and Rome in Italy.

The European Christians eventually reacted by waging a series of wars, called Crusades, against Islam between the 11th and 13th centuries. Their purpose was to recapture their Holy Land, where Christ and the first Christians had lived and taught. But other important issues were also at stake, including territory and trade. The Christians only enjoyed temporary successes, such as the capture of Antioch in 1098 (left). In the early days of Islam, the Muslims had been tolerant of Christians, but the Crusades created a deep distrust which was to affect travel across the Middle East for centuries.

THE MONGOLS AND MARCO POLO

During the early 13th century the Mongols united under their leader Genghis Khan (about 1167–1227). They then swept into China and across northern Asia. By 1241 these ruthless warriors had created an empire that stretched to the borders of Europe.

Several European ambassadors were dispatched to talk to the Mongol leaders. There was a hope that they might be persuaded to join Christian Europe in its fight against the Islamic Empire.

In the 1260s two merchant brothers from Venice called Maffeo and Niccolò Polo went on a trading expedition across the Black Sea. Hostile Mongols prevented them from taking a direct route home, and in their effort to skirt around them they ended up in China. By 1265 they had reached Beijing, then called Khanbalik, where they were treated well by the Mongol emperor of China, Kublai Khan. They returned home in 1269, but decided to make another trip to China two years later. This time they took Niccolò's 17-year-old son, Marco, with them. It was to be one of the great voyages of exploration of all time, lasting 24 years in all. Many of their tales of the wealth and splendour they had seen were disbelieved.

Above The landscape of central Asia was a formidable barrier to travellers attempting to reach the East. Mountainous wastelands, which are hot deserts in summer and bitterly cold in winter, gave little hint of the magnificent civilizations that lay beyond them.

Right Marco Polo was treated with great favour by the emperor of China, Kublai Khan (about 1215–1294). He was the grandson of the great Genghis Khan.

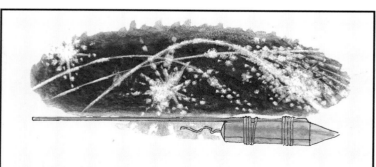

Marvels of China

Marco Polo came across many things in China which were quite unknown in Europe. The Chinese had invented gunpowder, which they used to make fireworks. They made printed books by using carved woodblocks. They even had paper money — an idea that seemed quite ridiculous to Europeans! Marco Polo also reported seeing mysterious 'black stones, which they dig out and burn like firewood': coal! When he wrote of such things, many people thought he was making them up.

Prester John

In medieval times the Christians of Europe believed in the legend of Prester John, the ruler of a lost Christian kingdom somewhere in Asia. If such a kingdom existed, they thought, it could help the Crusaders to defeat the Muslims by attacking from the east. A similar rumour suggested that one of the Mongol leaders might be Christian. Prester John was not to be found in Asia, and so it was thought that his kingdom must be in East Africa.

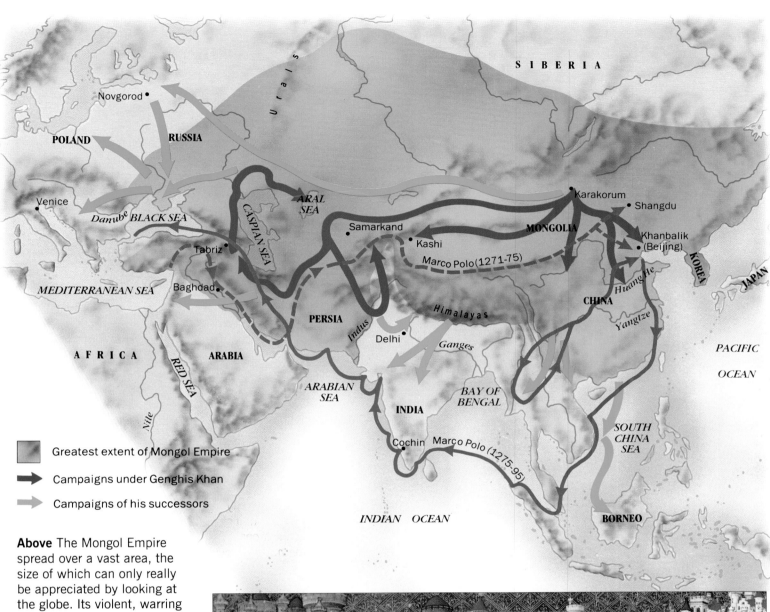

Greatest extent of Mongol Empire

Campaigns under Genghis Khan

Campaigns of his successors

Above The Mongol Empire spread over a vast area, the size of which can only really be appreciated by looking at the globe. Its violent, warring rulers presented a confusing picture to the Europeans, but as long as the trade routes were kept open they were happy to stay beyond its borders.

Marco Polo

Marco Polo set off from Venice with his father and uncle in 1271 (right), and they travelled for three and a half years to reach Shangdu (or Xanadu), the summer capital of Kublai Khan. The Emperor was much impressed by Marco and decided to make him his ambassador. Over a period of 17 years Marco travelled to various parts of the Empire. The Polos' return journey took another three years. They reached Venice in 1295. Marco Polo died in 1324.

THE QUEST FOR THE SPICE ISLANDS

Despite the reports of Marco Polo, it was not until the 15th century that the Portuguese began to make a determined effort to find the sources of the fabled riches of the East — in particular, spices.

In 1487 Pedro da Covilhã (see pages 46–47) reached India by crossing the Mediterranean and travelling down the Red Sea. What he found was a series of small independent states, many of which had become rich by trade with the Arab world.

Da Covilhã's reports made the Portuguese determined to find the sea route to the East. In 1498 Vasco da Gama became the first European explorer to reach India by sailing around the southern tip of Africa.

The Portuguese then began a series of aggressive naval expeditions. They established a fort on Sri Lanka in 1505 and captured Goa in 1510. But still they had not found the source of the spices, so they pushed on eastwards. In 1511 an expedition of three ships sailed from Portuguese-controlled Malacca under the leadership of António de Abreu, and in the following year they reached the Banda Islands. This opened up the route to the Moluccas, then the only source of nutmeg and cloves in the world. The Portuguese had at last found the fabled Spice Islands.

Now they headed north to China and by the 1540s they had become the first Europeans to reach Japan.

Above It was the lure of spices that brought the Europeans to Java and the other islands of South-East Asia, but local traders and fishermen had sailed these seas for thousands of years before they arrived.

Below The Portuguese arrival in India opened the way for other European nations to begin trading with India, particularly the French, the British and the Dutch (pictured here trading in Delhi).

Passage to India

In 1497 the Portuguese naval captain Vasco da Gama (about 1460–1524) was commissioned by his king to see if it was possible to reach India by using the route around the southern tip of Africa, which Bartolomeu Dias had discovered in 1487 (see pages 46–47). Departing from Lisbon with four ships and 170 men, he sailed to Malindi on the east coast of Africa and engaged the services of some Arab pilots. They guided him to the port of Calicut, on the south-west coast of India, which he reached in May 1498. The Muslim traders here, however, were unimpressed by the goods that da Gama had brought; furthermore, they did not like the idea of Christian Europeans interfering with their trade. None the less, da Gama was able to buy a few spices and other goods, proving that he had found the route to the East, and he returned to Portugal. Despite the fact that only 55 men out of the original 170 who had sailed with him survived, he was celebrated as a hero.

Da Gama made another trading expedition to India in 1502. In 1524 he returned to India as Viceroy to govern the new Portuguese colonies, but unfortunately he died soon after his arrival.

Tightening their grip

Malacca (today spelt Melaka) occupies a commanding position on the Strait of Malacca. Since a large proportion of Far Eastern trade passes through this channel, Malacca developed into one of the world's wealthiest trading ports.

In the early decades of the 16th century the Portuguese were determined to take control of the spice trade by force. Having captured Goa in India in 1510, Afonso de Albuquerque headed eastwards to Malacca, which he captured in 1511.

Soon the Portuguese had established their own colony in Malacca, and by the 1520s they had taken over the production of cloves and nutmeg (left) in the 'Spice Islands'.

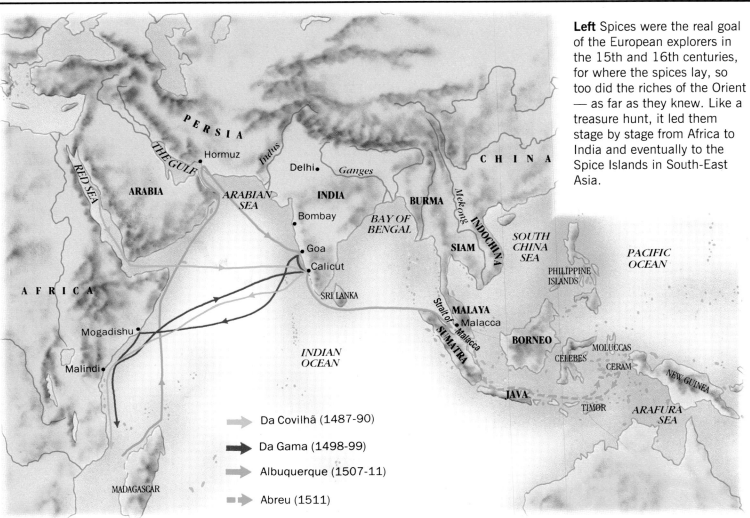

Left Spices were the real goal of the European explorers in the 15th and 16th centuries, for where the spices lay, so too did the riches of the Orient — as far as they knew. Like a treasure hunt, it led them stage by stage from Africa to India and eventually to the Spice Islands in South-East Asia.

→ Da Covilhã (1487-90)

→ Da Gama (1498-99)

→ Albuquerque (1507-11)

➡ Abreu (1511)

Precious spices

Spices originally grew only in southern Asia and South-East Asia. Cinnamon came from Sri Lanka; nutmeg and cloves came from the Moluccas; pepper came from various islands of South-East Asia; and ginger came mainly from China.

Spices are excellent trade goods. They are easy to handle and look after, and large quantities can be broken up into smaller and smaller portions for sale. In Europe they were used to preserve meat over winter and to flavour food, as well as to make medicines and perfumes. But before the Europeans had direct access to the places where they were grown, spices were very expensive. Once the European nations had control of the trade, prices began to drop.

REMOTE ASIAN LANDS

Much of central Asia and Japan remained beyond the reach of all but a few travellers for many centuries.

The Chinese were always suspicious of foreigners. The Ming Dynasty (1368–1644) turned its back on the outside world — apart from the brief spell under Emperor Ch'eng Tsu in the early 15th century (see pages 44–45).

The Portuguese had reached Japan in the 1540s, closely followed by missionaries, including St Francis Xavier. The Christian population of Japan grew to about 300 000 before a new *shogun* (feudal lord) called Tokugawa Ieyasu began to persecute them in about 1615. Foreigners were expelled and Japanese citizens were expressly forbidden from travelling abroad.

In central Asia and Tibet both the mountainous landscape and the hostility of governments stood in the way of exploration. Rare exceptions include some Christian missionaries who reached Tibet in 1611, and a Briton called Thomas Manning who reached Lhasa in 1811.

The French missionaries Abbé Huc and Joseph Gabet travelled through China in the most gruelling conditions to reach Tibet in 1846, only to be expelled after six weeks. Their book, *Travels in Tartary, Tibet and China,* excited the imagination of other explorers. But because of its inaccessibility, Tibet remained within the sights of only the most determined and persistent travellers until well into the 20th century.

Above The Potala Palace looms over Lhasa, the capital of Tibet, perched on a massive rock. This was the home of the Dalai Lama, or ruler of Tibet, until 1959.

Below The delicate architecture of this building in Kyoto, the capital of Japan until 1868, is an example of the unique qualities of Japanese culture.

'Apostle of the Indies'

St Francis Xavier (1506–1552) was a Spanish missionary who was one of the founders of the Roman Catholic Jesuit movement. He travelled to southern Asia, making numerous converts in Goa, Sri Lanka and the Moluccas, before reaching Japan in 1549.

Prayers on the wind

Travellers in the Himalayas have always been fascinated by the traditions of Tibetan Buddhism. Since their invasion of Tibet in 1950, the Chinese have destroyed many of the great monasteries there. But Buddhism lives on. Prayer flags and prayer wheels (below) are used in a constant round of prayers.

Above Travellers in the Himalayas face unusual challenges, from the weather as well as the mountainous landscape. Even today, in some areas there are no roads and traders, travellers, pilgrims and administrators have to use a network of ancient paths to travel between remote villages. Rivers may be spanned by bridges made of bamboo or rope which would deter all but the most dauntless traveller.

Parisian lady in Lhasa

In the 19th century the British controlled most of India, but they were always concerned about India's northern borders with the rest of Asia. In 1903 Sir Francis Younghusband, himself a great traveller of the region, arranged a treaty with the Tibetans to keep all non-British people out.

None the less, a French explorer called Alexandra David-Néel (1868–1969) wanted to visit Tibet, and being turned back by the British in 1912 only made her more determined. Guided by a Buddhist monk called Aphur Yongden, she spent 12 years travelling in Sikkim, Tibet and China, and studying Buddhism and the Tibetan language. Disguised as a poor Tibetan pilgrim, she eventually succeeded in reaching Lhasa in 1924. She was the first Western woman to have achieved this. Her account of her journey, *Travels of a Parisian Lady in Lhasa*, was published in 1928.

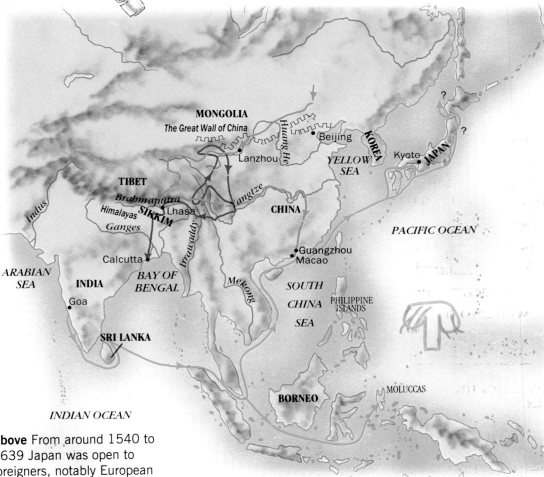

Above From around 1540 to 1639 Japan was open to foreigners, notably European missionaries. But after this it remained shut off from the rest of the world. Explorers were prevented from reaching the remote regions of the Himalayas, especially Tibet, by the awesome landscape, as well as by deliberate policy to keep them out.

⇨ Xavier and other Jesuits (1540-1622)

⇨ Abbé Huc (1844-46)

⇒ Alexandra David-Néel (1921-24)

THE NORTHEAST PASSAGE

By the 1570s the Portuguese and the Spanish were in control of the routes to the Far East across the southern oceans. Other European nations wanted to find sea-routes either westwards around the north of America (a route they called the Northwest Passage), or eastwards around the north of Russia (which they referred to as the Northeast Passage).

The first explorer to make a serious attempt to find the Northeast Passage was the Dutchman Willem Barents, who led three expeditions in the 1590s and reached Novaya Zemlya before being defeated by ice.

By the 1720s the Russians still did not know if their country was joined on to North America. The Danish explorer Vitus Bering (about 1680–1741) was commissioned to investigate. In 1728 he sailed between Russia and Alaska through the strait now named after him, but fog prevented him from being sure that this stretch of water separated Russia from North America.

The mapping of the northern seas over the next century proved that a Northeast Passage did exist. But the first man to sail along it was the Swedish Finn Baron Adolf Nordenkiöld in 1878–1879. Powerful ice-breaking ships were used to forge a route in 1910 and since the 1930s the Passage has been used regularly by Russian ships.

Below The land to the north of Russia lies well inside the Arctic Circle and is ice-bound for 10 months of the year.

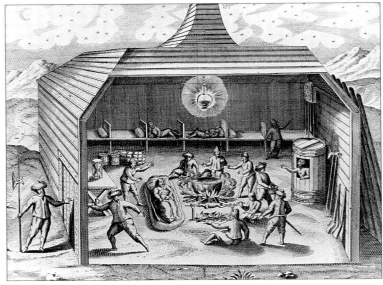

Above Barents' expedition spent the winter of 1596–1597 in a house built from the timbers of their ship. In June 1597 they set out for the south in open boats. Barents died, but 12 men survived.

Left In 1596 Barents reached Spitzbergen and crossed the sea now named after him to northern Novaya Zemlya. Here his ship was trapped and crushed by ice, as the Arctic winter set in.

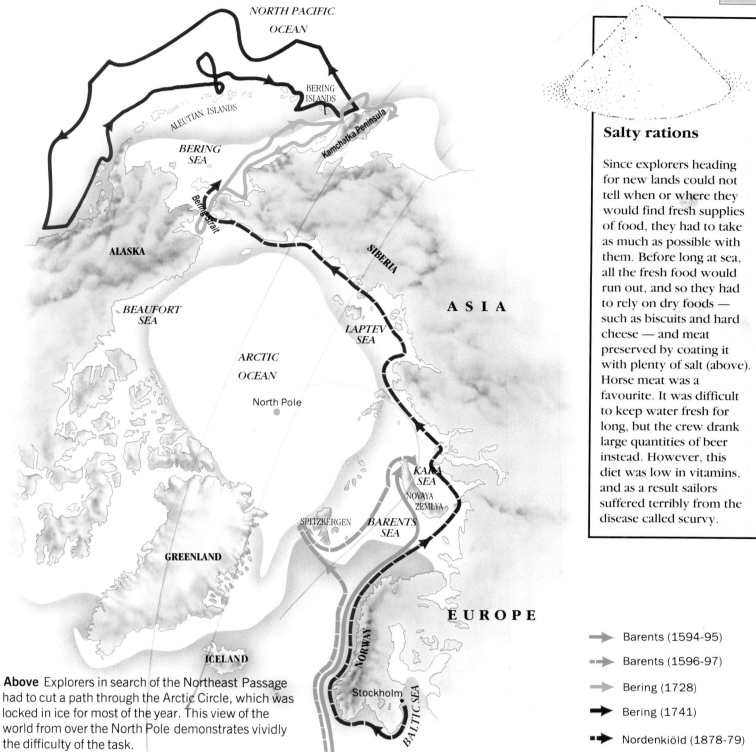

NORTH PACIFIC OCEAN

BERING ISLANDS

ALEUTIAN ISLANDS

Kamchatka Peninsula

BERING SEA

Bering Strait

ALASKA

SIBERIA

BEAUFORT SEA

LAPTEV SEA

ARCTIC OCEAN

ASIA

North Pole

KARA SEA

NOVAYA ZEMLYA

SPITZBERGEN

BARENTS SEA

GREENLAND

EUROPE

NORWAY

ICELAND

Stockholm

BALTIC SEA

Above Explorers in search of the Northeast Passage had to cut a path through the Arctic Circle, which was locked in ice for most of the year. This view of the world from over the North Pole demonstrates vividly the difficulty of the task.

➡ Barents (1594-95)
⇢ Barents (1596-97)
➡ Bering (1728)
➡ Bering (1741)
⇢ Nordenkiöld (1878-79)

Salty rations

Since explorers heading for new lands could not tell when or where they would find fresh supplies of food, they had to take as much as possible with them. Before long at sea, all the fresh food would run out, and so they had to rely on dry foods — such as biscuits and hard cheese — and meat preserved by coating it with plenty of salt (above). Horse meat was a favourite. It was difficult to keep water fresh for long, but the crew drank large quantities of beer instead. However, this diet was low in vitamins, and as a result sailors suffered terribly from the disease called scurvy.

Vitus Bering

Vitus Bering oversaw the Great Northern Expedition of 1733-1743 which mapped much of the coast of Siberia and Alaska. He himself mapped eastern Siberia and then the southern parts of Alaska with the intention of claiming Alaska for Russia. (Alaska was Russian until 1867 when it was sold to the United States.) However, Bering died of scurvy on the return journey in 1741.

The discovery of the Bering Strait suggested that this could be the possible exit for the Northeast Passage. It was also the exit for the Northwest Passage, but it was 100 years before this was proved by a British party led by Commander Robert McLure, which sailed northwards through the Bering Strait in 1850. After being rescued from disaster, the expedition was taken eastwards, reaching Baffin Bay in eastern Canada in 1854.

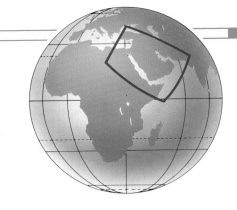

TRAVELS IN ARABIA

Since the Crusades during the Middle Ages, the Muslims of the Arab world looked upon outsiders from Christian Europe with great mistrust. Christian travellers were liable to be imprisoned, beaten or killed — especially if they tried to enter the holy cities of Islam such as Mecca and Medina. None the less, some brave travellers did succeed in reaching these places, including the Portuguese Pedro da Covilhã in 1492 (see pages 30–31).

During the early 19th century the European nations began to create various trading stations around the coasts of the Arabian peninsula, but the interior remained a blank on the map. The fact that so little was known about this region, or the people who lived there, meant that it began to excite great curiosity.

Arabia became an explorer's challenge. There were few rewards here in terms of trade or conquest: travellers in this region were usually scholars in a daring pursuit of knowledge, such as Johann Burckhardt or Charles Doughty; or scholar-adventurers in search of glory, such as Richard Burton and Harry St John Philby. To survive in this hostile environment, they usually had to study Arabic and Islam, and disguise themselves as Arab travellers. Even so they had to pay enormous attention to detail in all aspects of their speech and dress. Even the slightest mistake could mean detection and possible death.

The exploration of Arabia by Europeans took well over a century. The Empty Quarter, the most hostile part of the Arabian peninsula, remained unexplored until the 1930s.

A British adventurer

Richard Burton (1821–1890) was one of the outstanding explorers of the Victorian age. He had a wildly adventurous and unpredictable nature, but he was highly capable and had an exceptional gift for learning foreign languages. In 1853, while serving as an officer in the British Indian Army, he was given permission to travel in Arabia. Disguised as a Muslim doctor, he joined the pilgrimage to the sacred Muslim shrines of Mecca and Medina. Four years later he travelled to East Africa with Speke in search of the source of the Nile (see pages 50–51).

Desert dwellers

The Bedouin are nomadic people who have traditionally inhabited desert regions of the Middle East. (The word in Arabic means 'desert dwellers'.) They make their livelihood from their sheep and camels, moving their tents from place to place in search of pasture. They know exactly where water can be found, and can survive in the most difficult conditions where those who do not have their knowledge soon die.

Charles Doughty (1843–1926) lived and travelled with the Bedouin for eight months in 1876. He refused to disguise the fact that he was a Christian, and so was treated with suspicion. But he learnt a great deal about the hardships of their lives and their traditions of kindness and hospitality.

Doughty was in the Middle East for two years, and took a further 10 years to write up his notes. His book, *Travels in Arabia Deserta*, is one of the classics of travel writing.

A lost world carved in stone

Johann Burckhardt (1784–1817) was a Swiss scholar working in England, who was chosen by the African Association (see pages 48–49) to make an expedition across the Sahara Desert. He went to Syria in 1809 to learn Arabic and study Islam, then set off on an overland trip to Cairo. It was on this journey that he came across the ruins of the lost city of Petra (right), carved out of pink sandstone and hidden in a remote valley. This was once the capital of the Nabataeans, founded in the 4th century BC and an early centre for Christianity.

After reaching Cairo, he travelled south along the Nile where he discovered the now famous temple of Abu Simbel, then across the Red Sea to Mecca, disguised as an Egyptian Arab. He returned to Cairo in 1815, but died there in 1817.

Below European travellers had reached parts of the Muslim Arabian peninsula as early as the 15th century, and several had managed to infiltrate Mecca, the most sacred city of Islam. But the interior remained one of the last great challenges of Asian exploration.

Right During the First World War, T.E. Lawrence fought alongside the Arabs in their struggle against the Turks. His knowledge of the Arabs and their way of life became so great that he became known as Lawrence of Arabia.

The Queen of Sheba

According to legend, the Queen of Sheba visited King Solomon in the 10th century BC. The Old Testament says she came to seek the King's wisdom, but the most likely reason was to establish trade links. This temple, at Marib in Yemen, is said to commemorate her visit.

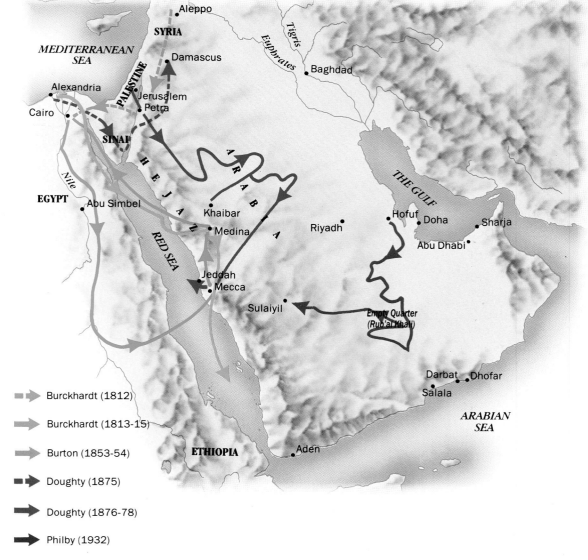

Burckhardt (1812)

Burckhardt (1813-15)

Burton (1853-54)

Doughty (1875)

Doughty (1876-78)

Philby (1932)

Africa has produced the earliest traces of human life, dating back to 3 or 4 million years ago. The Ancient Egyptians developed one of the first great civilizations. Yet Africa remained a mystery to the outside world.

THE FIRST HUMANS

Africa could claim to be the birthplace of humankind, from where early forms of human beings moved out to populate the rest of the world about 2 million years ago.

Much more recently, about 6 000 years ago, the fertile valley of the River Nile provided the right conditions for the civilization of Ancient Egypt to take root. By 2500 BC the first pyramids had been completed — some of the world's great marvels of engineering and the only one of the seven wonders of the ancient world still standing.

Yet the progress of civilization was to remain centred upon the Mediterranean and Asia. South of the Sahara traditions of herding, farming and trading never led to ambitious town-building, with rare exceptions such as Great Zimbabwe.

Meanwhile Arab, European, even Chinese traders found what they wanted around the coasts, and for centuries the heartlands of Africa remained virtually undisturbed by outsiders from other continents.

First of the line

The modern form of human beings (*Homo sapiens sapiens*) has only been in existence for 100 000 years. Since Darwin proposed that humans descended from ape-like ancestors (see pages 64–65), researchers have hoped to find the remains of earlier human forms. Traces of various hominids, the earliest human-like forms, such as this skull, have been found in East Africa. *Australopithecus afarensis* dates back about 4 million years. But *Homo habilis*, of 2 million years ago, is more likely to be the ancestor of modern human beings. Traces of *Homo habilis* have been found in the Olduvai Gorge in the Rift Valley of East Africa. *Homo habilis* was the first creature to use rough-cut flints for tools.

Above Great Zimbabwe was a major trading centre which flourished during the African Iron Age, between AD 1000 and 1450. The massive stone walls give some idea of the town. It was not until the 18th century that Europeans began to appreciate the potential that Africa held. By the mid-19th century the scramble for territory in Africa was at its height. Zimbabwe became part of the British Empire as Southern Rhodesia. When it achieved independence, it reverted to its original name.

Left The Sahara has always provided a barrier to travel, although trading caravans have crossed the desert for centuries. As a result, the people and cultures of North Africa have always remained separate from those to the south of the desert.

Below Archaeological finds in East Africa suggest that this was a centre for early forms of the human species. Human development generally followed a southward movement in Africa. The practice of cattle farming, then the use of iron, gradually spread throughout the continent from the Mediterranean coasts.

Above Some of Africa's finest works of art came from the kingdom of Benin, which flourished from the 13th to the 17th century.

Below The mud houses of the Dogon people of Mali demonstrate how traditional African life has survived in some of the inland parts of Africa.

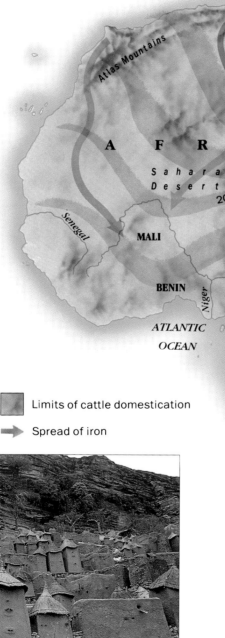

Limits of cattle domestication

Spread of iron

MEDITERRANEAN SEA

Atlas Mountains

A F R I C A

Sahara Desert

Thebes

RED SEA

Nile

4500 BC

3000 BC

2000 BC

1500 BC

Kingdom of Meroe 900 BC–AD 400

Early human migration

ARABIA

Senegal

MALI

BENIN

Niger

ATLANTIC OCEAN

Ethiopian Highlands

Zaire

500 BC

Lake Victoria

Great Rift Valley

Olduvai Gorge

INDIAN OCEAN

AD 500

Zambezi

AD 1000

Great Zimbabwe

Limpopo

MADAGASCAR

Kalahari Desert

Orange

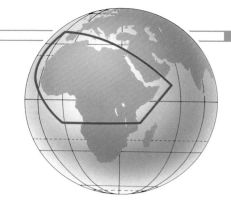

ANCIENT EGYPT

The civilization of Ancient Egypt developed over 5 000 years ago. It was centred upon the fertile and navigable stretches of the River Nile to the north of the First Cataract (a point on the river where waterfalls occur). This is part of the 'Fertile Crescent' which also saw the birth of civilizations in Mesopotamia, in the land between the Tigris and Euphrates rivers.

Ancient Egypt developed links with the other kingdoms and peoples of the Middle East, but expeditions to the rest of Africa lying to the south seem to have been few and far between. The rare exceptions were recorded in elaborate inscriptions. A famous example is a major expedition carried out under the orders of Queen Hatshepsut in 1492 BC to the 'Land of Punt', which is believed to be somewhere in the region of modern Somalia.

At various times Phoenicia came within the Empire of Egypt. In about 600 BC, Pharaoh Necho II commissioned a Phoenician fleet to find a route from the Red Sea to the Mediterranean. They appear to have achieved this by sailing around the Cape of Good Hope. They reported seeing the sun on their right as they travelled from east to west around the southern tip of Africa — but because people living in the Northern Hemisphere would have had no experience of this, many disbelieved their story.

The Phoenicians were the great seamen of their time, and had travelled beyond the Strait of Gibraltar to Madeira and the Canary Islands by the 7th century BC, where they traded in dye. General Hanno, from Carthage, led a huge fleet in this direction in 470 BC and continued his journey down much of the west coast of Africa.

The story of the expedition to Punt is told in a series of inscriptions (left) on the walls of Deir el-Bahri (above), the vast temple to the west of Thebes built by the powerful Queen Hatshepsut (reigned 1501–1479 BC). The inscriptions seen here show living myrrh trees arriving in Thebes — presumably after being carried in their pots from the Red Sea to the River Nile.

The voyage to Punt

Like many journeys of exploration that have taken place since, the expedition to the Land of Punt in 1492 BC was primarily concerned with trade. Records of the expedition speak glowingly of the vast quantities of goods brought back by the ships of the expedition, pictured fully laden on the walls of Deir el-Bahri (right). These included incense, ebony, ivory, gold

The world's first explorer?

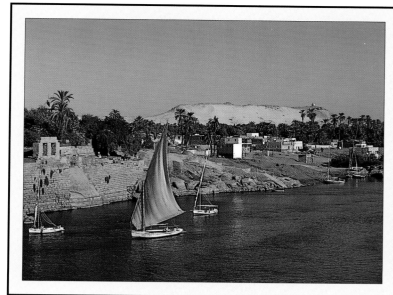

In about 2300 BC an official called Harkhuf was sent on expeditions to Yam, in Nubia. By travelling beyond the First Cataract of the River Nile, he crossed the furthest limit of the known world of the Ancient Egyptians. A record of his journeys was found in inscriptions on his tomb at Elephantine Island (left), on the Nile.

Sacred cargoes

The Ancient Egyptians preserved the bodies of their dead by embalming them with various salts, resins, oils and ointments — a process overseen by the jackal-headed god Anubis. Many of the precious substances they used in the process, such as myrrh and frankincense, had to be imported from abroad.

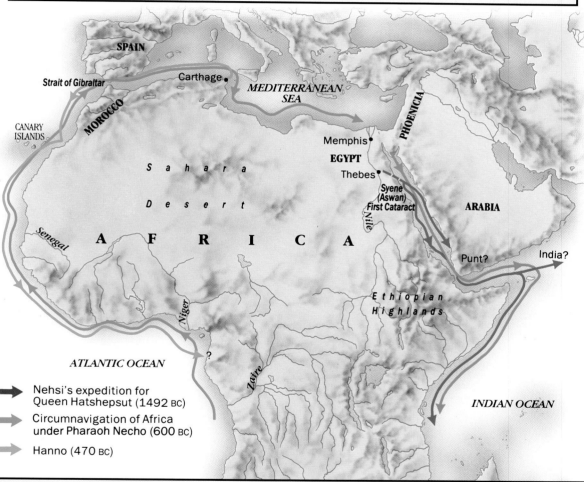

SPAIN

Strait of Gibraltar

CANARY ISLANDS

MOROCCO

Carthage

MEDITERRANEAN SEA

PHOENICIA

Memphis

EGYPT

Thebes

Syene (Aswan) First Cataract

Nile

ARABIA

Punt?

India?

S a h a r a D e s e r t

A F R I C A

Senegal

Niger

Ethiopian Highlands

ATLANTIC OCEAN

Zaire

?

INDIAN OCEAN

➤ Nehsi's expedition for Queen Hatshepsut (1492 BC)

➤ Circumnavigation of Africa under Pharaoh Necho (600 BC)

➤ Hanno (470 BC)

Left Given the time span of a thousand years, the progress of Egyptian exploration was slow, and focused primarily on the coasts of Africa and the pursuit of trade. Even Pharaoh Necho's daring expedition around Africa was inspired by his wish to find a trade route that could link the Red Sea to the Nile Delta.

and silver, and live monkeys.

The expedition would have travelled overland from Thebes to join ocean-going ships on the Red Sea, which then sailed about 2 000 km (1 250 miles) down the Red Sea to Punt. The astonished reaction of the people of Punt, recorded in the inscriptions at Deir el-Bahri, indicates that this was genuinely a journey of exploration, not a regular trading mission.

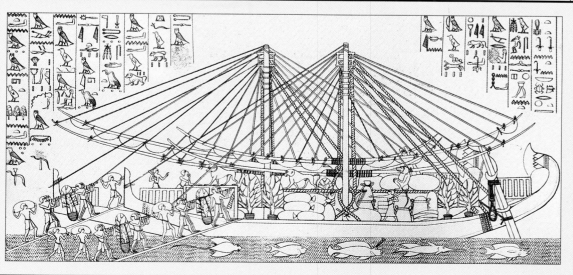

ARAB TRAVELLERS IN AFRICA

Within 70 years of the death of the Prophet Muhammad (see pages 26–27), Islam had spread across the length of North Africa bringing the Arab influence to Egypt, Libya, Tunisia, Algeria and Morocco.

The Arabs were quick to exploit the trading routes from North Africa to West Africa, travelling across the Sahara from oasis to oasis in caravans of camels. With trade came Islam, and these caravan routes were soon used by Muslim pilgrims on their way to and from Mecca, a journey that could take five or more years. One pilgrim from North Africa was Ibn Battuta (1304–1377), who was celebrated as the most widely travelled man of his day.

By the 13th century West Africa had become the world's most important source of gold. Several travellers reported on the fabulous wealth of Timbuktu, and for European adventurers Timbuktu became legendary. But it took them 300 years to reach it.

Above Ibn Battuta wrote his accounts of his journeys in Fez, Morocco, where he settled at the end of his travels after his journey to West Africa. A major trading centre, Fez is famous for its dye-works, where wool is still dyed in traditional open-air vats. It is also a centre of Islamic learning, with one of the world's oldest universities, founded in AD 850.

Below The Arabs were skilled traders, and for centuries controlled all trade between Asia and Europe, much of which came up the Red Sea and then overland to Alexandria. In West Africa they exchanged salt and various luxury goods for gold and slaves. The routes across the Sahara were difficult and dangerous, but the rewards were great. Merchants such as these could make great fortunes on one trip alone.

Ships and ships of the desert

Ibn Battuta (1304–1377) was born in Tangier, Morocco. In 1325 he decided to make the pilgrimage to Mecca — the start of some 30 years of travel. His route took him to Jerusalem and Damascus, where he became a teacher of Islam. After studying law in Mecca, he began a series of journeys which took him to the most far-flung places of the world that had been reached by Islam. He sailed down the Red Sea to East Africa, then went north to the Black Sea and on to India and China. He joined a trading caravan across the western Sahara to West Africa, travelling with 'ships of the desert' — camels. After his final return to Morocco in 1354 he had travelled 120 700 km (75 000 miles).

Islam in Africa

As in India and South-East Asia, Islam spread to East and West Africa mainly through trade, not conquest. Islam also spread down the River Nile to Sudan, and to the countries to the south of the Sahara. It reached West Africa by the caravan routes across the Sahara.

Islam was adopted by the Mali Empire after AD 1000. The wealth of these West African Muslims became famous: in 1324 King Mansa Musa took so much gold with him on his pilgrimage to Mecca that he unbalanced the economies of countries on his route.

Islam is still a strong force in Africa today, as witnessed by the men (right) attending prayers at a mosque in Burkina.

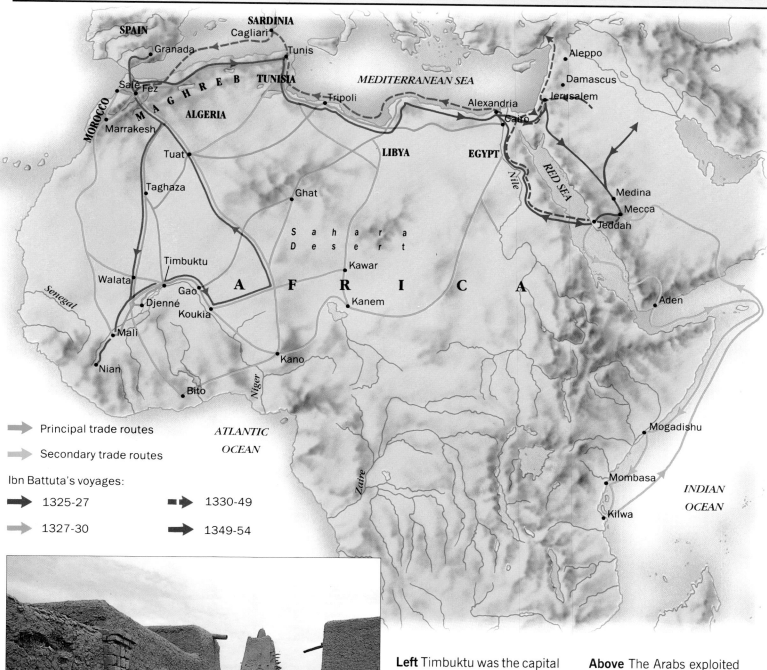

Principal trade routes

Secondary trade routes

Ibn Battuta's voyages:

1325-27

1327-30

1330-49

1349-54

Left Timbuktu was the capital of the Mali Empire in the 14th century and grew rich on trade in salt and gold. After being sacked by the Moroccans in 1593, however, it went into decline, by which time it had acquired legendary status among Europeans.

Above The Arabs exploited established trade links across the Sahara to the nations of West Africa. These routes were used by explorers in the 14th century, and European explorers 500 years later. Ibn Battuta also made advantage of the sea routes used by Arab traders.

ACROSS THE INDIAN OCEAN

As early as the 9th century, East Africa had trading connections that stretched to the Arab world, India, to South-East Asia, and even China. Arab merchants had settled in the ports, such as Zanzibar, where they traded in ivory, rhinoceros horn, gold and slaves, receiving in return spices, silks and Chinese porcelain, some of which they traded with Europeans.

Chinese merchants were known to have visited the Middle East by sea as early as AD 360, and had certainly reached Zanzibar and Madagascar by the 1180s. However, these were exceptions. The Chinese were only able to explore beyond their own borders during certain periods of their history.

One of these periods occurred under Emperor Ch'eng Tsu in the early Ming Dynasty (1368–1644). He put a Muslim courtier, Admiral Cheng Ho, or Zheng Ho (1371–1435), in charge of a massive fleet, and this undertook a series of seven voyages of exploration from 1405 to 1433. They had reached Africa by 1415. They may even have rounded the Cape of Good Hope — some 70 years before the first Europeans did so.

Above Zanzibar was one of several wealthy trading ports on the East African coast where Arab traders settled, bringing Islam with them. Arabs were the chief slave traders until the 19th century.

Below This picture of a Chinese man leading a zebra dates from 1430. A number of African animals reached China during the period of Cheng Ho's voyages, usually as gifts to the emperor.

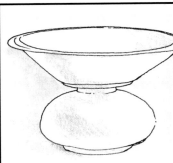

Precious china

The Chinese had mastered the technique of producing a kind of pottery called porcelain by the 10th century. It was made from a mixture of clays then found only in China, and was finer than any other pottery in the world. As a result it became highly prized, and was laboriously carried across Asia on the Silk Road (see pages 22–23) to Europe, and across the Indian Ocean to Africa. Pieces of porcelain have been found in the old Arab trading port of Kilwa on the East African coast.

After the Dutch East India Company came to dominate the trade in the 17th century, tonnes of Chinese porcelain were shipped all over the world. Europe started to produce its own porcelain in the 18th century.

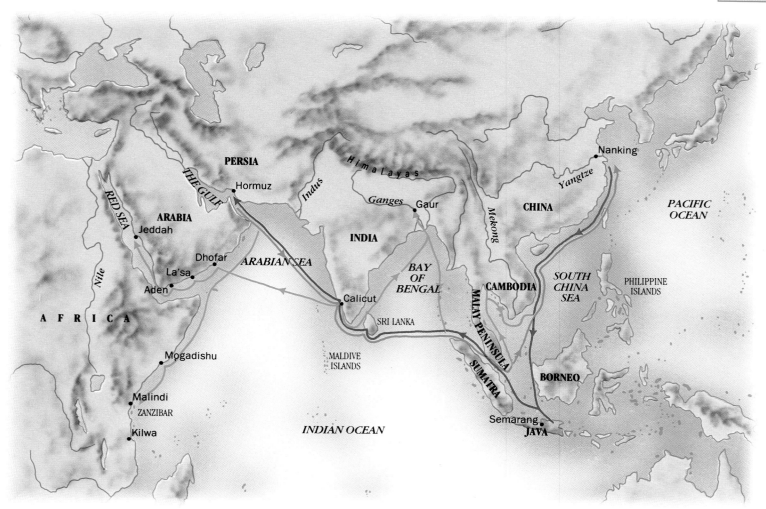

Cheng Ho's journeys

outward (1431-33)

return (1433)

additional voyages

Above Cheng Ho's epic journeys from 1405 to 1433 pieced together the numerous trading links that spanned the southern oceans.

Below Cheng Ho's fleet consisted mainly of junks. Some of these were five times the size of the Portuguese caravels.

Cheng Ho

Cheng Ho's fleet was probably the largest that ever sailed in the name of exploration. He was in command of 27 000 men and 317 ships, and his expeditions consisted of as many as 63 ships sailing together. His seven voyages lasted about two years each. The fleet travelled through much of South-East Asia, visiting ports such as Semarang (above), in Java, and perhaps even sailing to the north coast of Australia. Other expeditions went to India, the Gulf and the east coast of Africa. Their purpose was to trade, to collect taxes from Chinese colonies, and to gather information.

After Emperor Ch'eng Tsu died, Cheng Ho fell from favour. He was allowed to make one more voyage ending in 1433 before China once more turned its back on the outside world. One hundred years later the Europeans had explored much of the world which Cheng Ho had reached. If Cheng Ho's achievements had been maintained the history of exploration might have been different.

EARLY EUROPEAN EXPLORERS

During the first decades of the 15th century, the Portuguese began a series of voyages down the west coast of Africa in their search for a sea-route to the Far East. In 1434 Gil Eannes became the first navigator to dare to sail south of Cape Bojador. Fifty years later, in 1487, Bartolomeu Dias rounded the Cape of Good Hope, the tip of southern Africa.

That same year, Pedro da Covilhã and Afonso da Paiva crossed the Mediterranean and travelled down the Red Sea. Da Paiva went in search of Prester John in East Africa (see pages 28–29), but disappeared. Da Covilhã reached India, and later went to live in Abyssinia (Ethiopia). Meanwhile, in 1497 Vasco da Gama sailed up the east coast of Africa and finally found the sea-route to India (see pages 30–31) which European adventurers had been hoping to discover for many years.

On the way to the East, the Portuguese discovered the rich trading possibilities of West Africa — particularly in gold, ivory and slaves. The slave trade grew enormously between the 16th and 19th centuries, creating an atmosphere of fear and mistrust right across Africa that affected all later exploration of that vast continent.

Hope for the future

The rocky headland on the south-west tip of Africa was named the Cape of Storms by Bartolomeu Dias in 1487. But it was renamed the Cape of Good Hope by the Portuguese King John II, as it appeared to hold out the hope of a sea-route to the Far East. Ten years passed before this sea-route was confirmed by the Portuguese navigator Vasco da Gama who rounded the Cape in 1497.

Left The Portuguese navigator Diogo Gomes reached the Gulf of Guinea in 1458, opening up the route for European traders. This carved door panel, made by the Yoruba people of Nigeria, shows a Portuguese trader on horseback.

Right Maps made in the middle of the 16th century could show the coasts of Africa in detail. By contrast, the interior of Africa was virtually unknown. The spoke-like lines are an alternative to latitude and longitude: navigators could use them to work out their position.

Right The Portuguese progressed around Africa in a series of small steps, then giant leaps. The ultimate goal was always the spices of the East, but they soon recognized the trading opportunities of Africa itself.

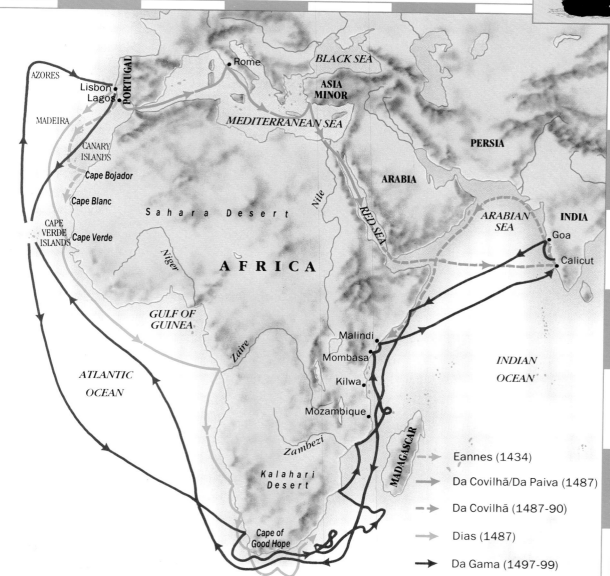

AZORES
PORTUGAL
Lisbon
Lagos
MADEIRA
CANARY ISLANDS
Cape Bojador
Cape Blanc
CAPE VERDE ISLANDS
Cape Verde
Niger
ATLANTIC OCEAN
GULF OF GUINEA
Zaïre
Kalahari Desert
Zambezi
Cape of Good Hope
Sahara Desert
Nile
AFRICA
RED SEA
ARABIA
MEDITERRANEAN SEA
Rome
BLACK SEA
ASIA MINOR
PERSIA
ARABIAN SEA
INDIA
Goa
Calicut
Malindi
Mombasa
Kilwa
Mozambique
MADAGASCAR
INDIAN OCEAN

→ Eannes (1434)
→ Da Covilhã/Da Paiva (1487)
⇢ Da Covilhã (1487-90)
→ Dias (1487)
→ Da Gama (1497-99)

Golden Guinea

Some West African countries became known by the most valuable trade goods found there. The British named a gold coin after the country from which the gold came: Guinea.

Below The Portuguese first set up trading posts along the coast of Africa, and then they built forts to protect them. The well-preserved thick walls of Fort Jesus in Mombasa, on the Kenyan coast of East Africa, show the typical architecture of Portuguese forts of the time.

Right When Vasco da Gama reached Mombasa in 1498 he was given a hostile reception, but was made welcome in Malindi, further north. Here he managed to recruit Arab pilots to guide his ships to India (see pages 30-31) where he landed at Calicut in May of that year and found trade was controlled by Muslims.

Left The great rivers of Africa — such as the Niger — became a major theme of exploration in the 19th century. Mapmakers needed to know where these rivers began and ended — but it was an obsession that often puzzled local people.

MAPPING THE RIVER NIGER

The west coast of Africa was famed for its riches in gold and ivory. Until the very end of the 18th century, however, all that European geographers knew of what lay beyond the coasts was that much of this wealth was traded along a great river called the Niger, and that the fabled city of Timbuktu lay on or near that river. Quite where the River Niger flowed from and to remained a mystery. Some people even speculated that it might be attached to the River Nile.

In 1788 the Association for Promoting the Discovery of Interior Parts of Africa (the African Association for short) was founded by Sir Joseph Banks, the naturalist who had accompanied Captain Cook (see pages 74–75). Its main aim was to encourage scientific exploration in Africa. It set its sights on West Africa and the River Niger, and sent the explorer Mungo Park on two expeditions there in 1795 and 1805.

Mungo Park died when close to unravelling the mystery of the Niger. His work was only completed in 1830 when the British brothers Richard and John Lander travelled by canoe from Bussa to the mouth of the river. However, Park's courage, determination, scientific thoroughness and kindliness became a model for 19th-century exploration which, sadly, few European explorers succeeded in living up to.

Left In the 1820s the Geographical Society of Paris offered a prize of 10 000 francs to the first person to reach Timbuktu — and return alive. A British army officer, Alexander Gordon Laing, reached it in 1826, but was murdered there. The prize was won by a Frenchman, René Caillié (1799–1838), who travelled from Senegal to Timbuktu in 1827–1828, disguised as an Egyptian Muslim. Then, to reach home, he crossed the Sahara with a camel caravan.

Timbuktu was a great disappointment to Caillié. He found little sign of the wealthy gold-trading centre it once had been (see pages 42–43).

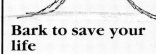

Bark to save your life

Malaria, a disease transmitted by mosquitoes, was responsible for countless deaths among the early explorers. In the 1850s and 1860s, however, a doctor working on the River Niger called William Baikie found that regular doses of quinine could protect people from malaria.

Quinine is made from the bark of the chinchona tree that grows in the Andes. The word comes from the Quechua Indian word *kina*, meaning bark.

Right Djenné, in modern Mali, was founded on a tributary of the River Niger in the 8th century and grew into a wealthy trading town and an important centre for Islamic learning.

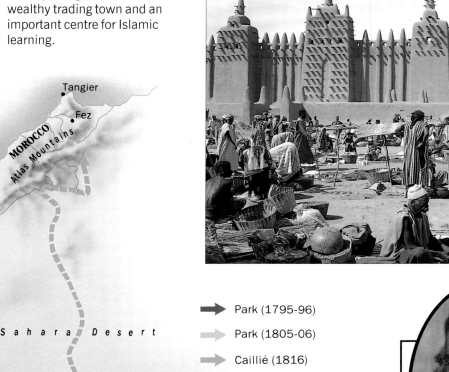

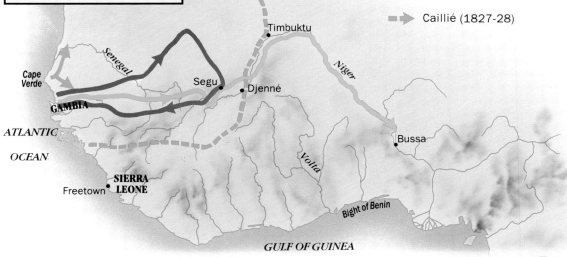

→ Park (1795-96)

→ Park (1805-06)

→ Caillié (1816)

⇢ Caillié (1827-28)

Heroism and tragedy

Mungo Park (1771–1806), a young Scottish doctor, was chosen by the African Association to undertake their first expedition to West Africa: to explore the River Niger. He set off from Gambia in 1795. Despite being abandoned by his African companions and imprisoned by Arabs for four months, he reached the Niger, and established that it flows eastwards.

In 1805 Park returned to the Niger as leader of a large expedition. He travelled much of the length of the river, but the expedition was a disaster. Most of its members died of disease and Park himself was killed in an ambush at Bussa when the rest of his team died with him.

Left Explorers faced huge difficulties crossing the interior of West Africa. Tropical forest cloaks much of the landscape. After centuries of disruption by the slave trade, local tribes were constantly at war and often hostile, and Europeans had little defence against tropical diseases, such as malaria and dysentery. West Africa soon became known as the 'white man's grave', but this did not stop European governments from having a greedy eye to territorial expansion. By the 19th century the entire area was controlled by Britain, France, Germany or Portugal.

Above Compared to the journeys of, say, Ibn Battuta in the 14th century (see pages 42–43), the achievements of the first European explorers in West Africa may look modest — but the distances covered are a measure of the extremely difficult conditions in which they travelled. These were, none the less, important early steps in the European exploration of the African interior.

THE SOURCE OF THE NILE

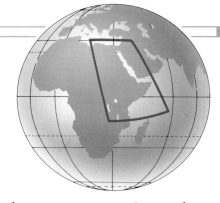

The great River Nile has been the subject of fascination since ancient times. But where did it flow from? How long was it? Ptolemy (see pages 10–11) suggested that it flowed from lakes in the 'Mountains of the Moon' in East Africa. The Romans sent an expedition up the Nile, but they only got as far as the swamplands of modern-day southern Sudan which are known as the Sudd.

By the 1850s much of northern and western Africa had been visited by explorers such as the German Heinrich Barth (1821–1865), who from 1849 to 1855 travelled across the Sahara to West Africa on a British expedition. The source of the Nile, however, remained a tantalizing mystery which many explorers were keen to solve.

In 1856 Richard Burton (see pages 36–37) set out from Zanzibar with John Hanning Speke (1827–1864) to try to solve this mystery. Speke reached Lake Victoria, which he declared to be the source of the Nile. But his observations did not prove this. In 1860–1862 Speke travelled again to Lake Victoria, this time with James Grant (1827–1892). Again their results were inconclusive.

They happened, by chance, to meet Samuel and Florence Baker who were on their way up the Nile from Khartoum. Together they had covered almost the entire length of the Nile. But there was still uncertainty about an unexplored stretch of the river between Lake Victoria and Lake Albert. It was Henry Morton Stanley (see pages 52–53) who finally, after years of speculation, proved that Lake Victoria is indeed the source of the Nile.

Burton and Speke

In 1856 Burton and Speke, both officers in the British Indian Army, were sent in search of the source of the River Nile by the Royal Geographical Society. After suffering great hardship and illness, they reached Lake Tanganyika in 1858. Speke then headed off alone and reached Lake N'yanza (right), which he renamed Lake Victoria after his queen. He was sure that this was the source of the Nile, but he failed to investigate it properly. This infuriated Burton, especially when, back in England, he found that Speke was being celebrated as the discoverer of the source of the River Nile.

After Speke's second expedition of 1860–1862, with Grant, Burton was still sure that Speke had not proved that Lake Victoria was the source of the Nile. In 1864 the Royal Geographical Society invited Burton and Speke to settle the issue in an open debate. However, Speke was mysteriously killed in a shooting accident the day before the debate was due to open.

Above The Nile is the longest river in the world at 6 695 km (4 160 miles). The White Nile flows from Lake Victoria and the shorter Blue Nile flows from Ethiopia. They come together at Khartoum, Sudan, to form one river. This picture shows the Nile as it flows past Elephantine Island near the First Cataract - one of a series of water rushes on the river. Excavations on the island have revealed carvings and inscriptions which have helped historians build up an extensive picture of what life was like in Ancient Egypt.

South of the Fifth Cataract is the confluence of the Blue and White Nile. The origin of the Blue Nile was discovered in 1613. The source of the White Nile was not discovered for almost another 250 years.

A Scotsman in Africa

In 1763, James Bruce, a Scottish wine merchant, was appointed British consul in Algiers. During his five years there he studied Arabic before setting off on his travels. He journeyed to Cairo and then to Ethiopia. He travelled to the headstream of the Blue Nile before returning along the Nile to Egypt, and then back to Britain where, sadly, he was ignored.

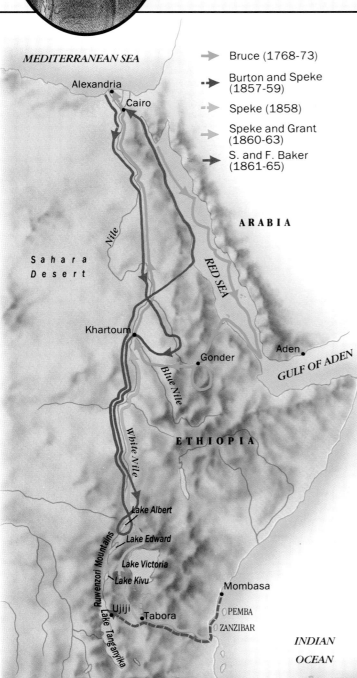

MEDITERRANEAN SEA

→ Bruce (1768-73)

→ Burton and Speke (1857-59)

→ Speke (1858)

→ Speke and Grant (1860-63)

→ S. and F. Baker (1861-65)

Alexandria
Cairo
ARABIA
Nile
RED SEA
Sahara Desert
Khartoum
Aden
Gonder
GULF OF ADEN
Blue Nile
White Nile
ETHIOPIA
Lake Albert
Lake Edward
Ruwenzori Mountains
Lake Victoria
Lake Kivu
Mombasa
Ujiji
Tabora
PEMBA
ZANZIBAR
Lake Tanganyika
INDIAN OCEAN

Left Bruce's achievements in East Africa in 1768-1773 were sufficient to make the African Association turn its attention to West Africa in 1795. It was another 75 years before the explorers focused on the Nile again.

Below Samuel White Baker (1821–1893) was a wealthy traveller and game hunter. In 1861 he set off up the Nile from Cairo. He met Speke and Grant in Gondokoro, then in 1864 reached and named Lake Albert. He was accompanied on his Nile expedition by his young Hungarian wife, Florence, whom he had bought in a Turkish slave market in Bulgaria.

The fly in the ointment

The European expeditions into Africa became increasingly ambitious in the late 19th century, and explorers travelled with an enormous quantity of baggage. They took clothes, tents and camp beds, food and cooking equipment, navigational instruments, arms and ammunition, and gifts for the African chiefs they encountered during their expeditions.

In other parts of the world they might have used horses or mules. In East Africa this was not possible because the tsetse fly spreads a disease which kills pack animals. Instead, porters were hired to carry the equipment.

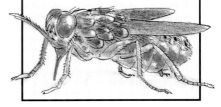

EXPLORING THE HEART OF AFRICA

Below In 1855 Livingstone became the first European to set eyes on the mighty Victoria Falls on the River Zambezi.

Up until the 1850s, very little was known about the interior of Africa by the world outside. Various European nations had well-established trading stations and settlements on the coasts but the rest was uncharted territory.

The Scottish missionary David Livingstone began his journey into the heart of Africa in 1849, when he travelled north from southern Africa across the Kalahari Desert and reached Lake Ngami. Between 1853 and 1856 he walked right across Africa. In 1865 he was sent by the Royal Geographical Society to look for the source of the Nile which was still disputed despite Speke's discoveries. In 1866, however, he disappeared around Lake Nyasa (now Lake Malawi) and there were no reports of him for three years.

In 1871 the journalist Henry Morton Stanley succeeded in finding him, sick but alive. This famous meeting inspired Henry Stanley to make two more major expeditions in Africa between 1874 and 1889.

Following in the footsteps of the explorers, almost all the European nations began to claim territory in Africa, justifying their action by stating that Africans would benefit from education and Christianity. Few people in Europe saw any wrong in this. Mary Kingsley, however, objected strongly. In 1895 she completed an extraordinarily courageous journey in western Africa, and her experiences led her to believe that traditional African ways of life should be respected and not interfered with. She was pointing the way towards the more sensitive kinds of exploration and anthropology of the 20th century, but her views were not accepted at the time.

Explorer with a mission

David Livingstone (1813–1873) was a trained doctor and a Christian missionary. He was sent to South Africa in 1841 where he believed himself called to take the Gospel to tribes living in the lands to the north. By opening up the interior of Africa to missionary work and different forms of trade, he hoped to put an end to slavery — a point made clear by the title page of a biography (right) published in 1878. Through his goodwill, he won the affection and loyalty of his African companions. After his death from dysentery by Lake Tanganyika, two of them carried his body 1 600 km (992 miles) to Zanzibar so that it could be shipped to London. In Britain he was buried in Westminster Abbey and was mourned as a national hero.

Livingstone made detailed records of his travels, including a sketch map of his idea of the sources of the Nile. His maps and journals were extremely valuable to European geographers, who had few other sources of information about the region.

Alone among cannibals

Mary Kingsley (1862–1900) made two journeys to the west coast of Africa, in 1893 and 1895. She earned particular fame for her journey among the hostile Fang people, winning their respect by showing bravery, and by interesting them in trade goods such as knives and cloth.

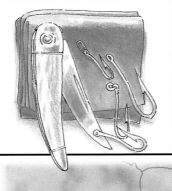

Below Livingstone and Stanley explored and mapped much of the interior of southern Africa over three decades. Mary Kingsley's journeys were on a much less grand scale.

Above The journeys of Livingstone and Stanley caught the public's imagination, as this Victorian board game shows. It paints a colourful but unrealistic picture.

The workhouse boy

Henry Morton Stanley (1841–1904) started life in a workhouse for the poor in Wales. His real name was John Rowlands. When still a boy he ran away to the United States. He was adopted by a wealthy man called Henry Morton Stanley, and he changed his name in his benefactor's honour. He became a successful journalist, and in 1871 he was sent by the editor of the *New York Herald* to discover what had happened to David Livingstone, whose exploits had captured the imagination of the American public. This was the start of his life as an explorer.

In 1874 he travelled from Zanzibar to Lake Victoria and proved that this was the source of the River Nile. He continued westwards, sailing down the River Lualaba and the River Congo (now Zaire), reaching the west coast after a journey lasting 999 days. He led one further expedition, to southern Sudan, in 1887–1889.

All of Stanley's expeditions were on an enormous scale, involving hundreds of guides and porters travelling long distances in very hazardous conditions. When he crossed Africa in 1874–1877, for example, Stanley set out with 356 people; only 115 of these reached the west coast.

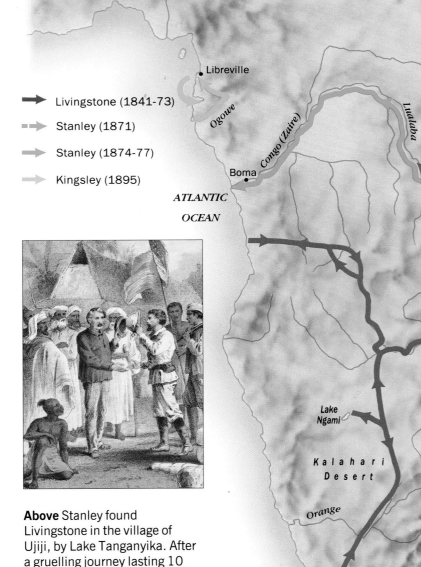

→ Livingstone (1841-73)
⇢ Stanley (1871)
→ Stanley (1874-77)
→ Kingsley (1895)

ATLANTIC OCEAN

Libreville
Ogowe
Congo (Zaire)
Boma
Lualaba
Lake Victoria
Ujiji • Tabora
Lake Tanganyika
ZANZIBAR
Dar es Salaam
INDIAN OCEAN
Lake Bangweulu
Lake Nyasa
Zambezi
Limpopo
Lake Ngami
Kalahari Desert
Orange
Cape Town

Above Stanley found Livingstone in the village of Ujiji, by Lake Tanganyika. After a gruelling journey lasting 10 months, he greeted Livingstone with the famous phrase: 'Dr Livingstone, I presume.'

SECTION 5: THE AMERICAS

The first Europeans arrived in South and Central America in 1492. They quickly realized this 'New World' offered land to conquer and to claim for themselves. For the people already living there, European exploration was to bring tragedy and destruction.

MOVING SOUTH

The first inhabitants of America crossed over from Asia around 25 000 years ago. When a corridor opened up to the east of the Rocky Mountains at the end of the last Ice Age around 12 000 years ago, they pushed down towards the temperate plains of North America and the warmer and much more hospitable lands further south.

North America was inhabited mainly by farmers and semi-nomadic hunters, while town-building civilizations developed in Central America as early as 1000 BC. The Mayas came to rule much of Central America until their Empire collapsed in about AD 900, when the Toltecs became dominant. They in turn were pushed out in the 13th century by the Aztecs when they invaded the Valley of Mexico.

Meanwhile, in the Andes mountains of South America, several early civilizations developed, and in the 15th century they were brought under the rule of the Incas.

Above The ancestors of the North American Indians were nomadic hunters. Gradually their lives became settled, and by 1000 BC most tribes grew much of their own food by farming the river valleys. Hunting remained an important part of life for many groups, however.

Below All the cultures of Central and South America built palaces and temples on a massive scale, often with giant sculptures to match. The Olmecs, who dominated Central America from 1200 to 400 BC, made huge stone heads using hammers made of very hard stone.

Making their mark

The territories of the Adena and Hopewell Indians of the central eastern part of North America were marked by huge mounds of earth which served as burial sites or as platforms for temples. Some mounds have precise geometric shapes, others represent animals such as birds or snakes, as at the Serpent Mound in Ohio, North America (above).

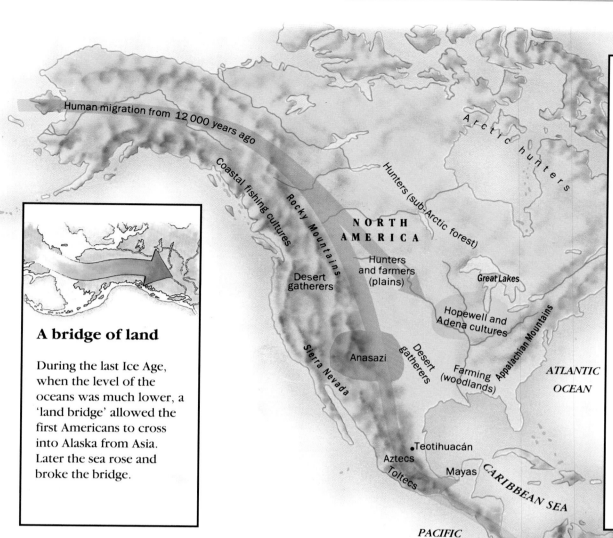

Human migration from 12 000 years ago

Coastal fishing cultures

Arctic hunters

Rocky Mountains

Hunters (sub-Arctic forest)

NORTH AMERICA

Hunters and farmers (plains)

Great Lakes

Desert gatherers

Hopewell and Adena cultures

Sierra Nevada

Anasazi

Desert gatherers

Farming (woodlands)

Appalachian Mountains

ATLANTIC OCEAN

•Teotihuacán

Aztecs

Toltecs

Mayas

CARIBBEAN SEA

PACIFIC OCEAN

Farmers (rain forest and savannah)

SOUTH AMERICA

Andes Mountains

Incas

Cuzco

•Tiahuanaco

Hunters (grasslands and savannah)

Fishing cultures

A bridge of land

During the last Ice Age, when the level of the oceans was much lower, a 'land bridge' allowed the first Americans to cross into Alaska from Asia. Later the sea rose and broke the bridge.

The golden touch

The people of the Andes were gifted craftsmen, with a unique way of portraying the world — as demonstrated by this pottery whistling bottle showing a man playing the Andean panpipes. They were also famous for their immense riches in gold, which they cast and sculpted into jewellery, ornaments and tools.

Above The Aztecs' colourful clothes and jewellery may have impressed the first European visitors but they lacked glass, iron, gunpowder and even the wheel.

Below By about AD 400 the Anasazi of south-west North America were living in villages built of stone or adobe (mud bricks). Later settlements were concealed in cliffs.

Above The first inhabitants of the Americas lived in the Arctic until the withdrawal of the ice cap 12 000 years ago allowed them to cross into the rest of North America. By about 2000 BC farming cultures were established.

55

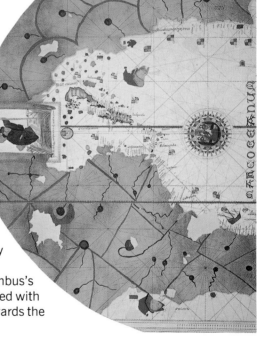

Left During Columbus's first voyage, a battle was fought between some of his men and local Indians on the island of Hispaniola. According to legend, the sky that day was full of arrows, hence this bay's name — The Bay of Arrows.

EUROPEAN ARRIVAL

In 1492 three small Spanish ships, the *Santa Maria*, the *Niña* and the *Pinta*, arrived on a tiny island of the Bahamas. Their leader, Christopher Columbus, named the island San Salvador (Holy Saviour). They were carrying the first Europeans to reach the Caribbean, and were the first of a new wave of European expeditions which would soon change the Americas for ever.

The Portuguese had been searching for a route to the Far East by pushing south down the coast of Africa. Columbus, by contrast, thought that it should be possible to reach the East by sailing westwards across the Atlantic. This is what Ptolemy's map (see pages 10–11) suggested. Unfortunately Ptolemy had underestimated the circumference of the world, so when Columbus reached San Salvador, he thought he had reached the Far East, and that the riches of China and India lay close by. He called the people living there 'Indians', and the islands the 'Indies'. This misnomer has persisted ever since.

Columbus made three more voyages, in 1493–1496, 1498–1500 and 1502–1504, visiting and naming many of the islands of the Caribbean, as well as the coasts of South and Central America. However, he never found the great quantities of gold he had dreamed of, and he never understood fully that he had not reached the Far East.

Right
This map, dated 1500, was drawn by Juan de la Cosa, who was with Columbus on his second voyage. It shows that most of the Caribbean had already been carefully charted by this time. St Christopher, Columbus's patron saint, is pictured with his head pointing towards the riches of the East.

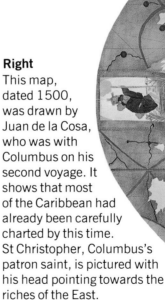

Hero and villain

Christopher Columbus, or Cristóbal Colón (1451–1506), was a weaver's son from Genoa in Italy. He was in the service of the Portuguese for about 10 years, but when the Portuguese king refused to support his plan to cross the Atlantic, he turned to King Ferdinand and Queen Isabella of Spain for assistance.

He was treated as a hero when he returned to Spain from his first expedition, and was made Governor of the

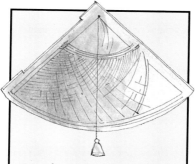

By the stars above

Christopher Columbus would undoubtedly have used a compass in his voyages across the Atlantic. Another instrument he would have used was the quadrant, which was a flat piece of wood or metal shaped like a quarter circle. A scale was drawn round the edge and when the instrument was held upright the navigator could work out a star's height above the horizon and, by using a star chart, could work out the ship's position.

Left 'Gold, God and Cathay [China]' were the reasons why Columbus wanted to reach the Far East. Queen Isabella of Spain was particularly attracted to the idea that Columbus would take Christianity to the people of the East. One of his first acts in San Salvador was to raise a cross.

Below Columbus's four voyages all led him to the same region of the Caribbean. They became progressively less rewarding as he ran into problems of colonization and administration. He remained convinced that he had discovered the Far East.

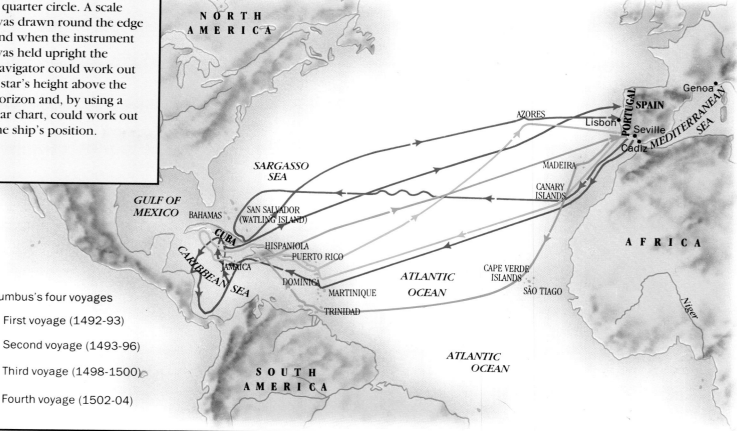

Columbus's four voyages

→ First voyage (1492-93)

→ Second voyage (1493-96)

→ Third voyage (1498-1500)

→ Fourth voyage (1502-04)

new islands which he had discovered. But he was clearly unsuited to these responsibilities. On later expeditions he treated the Spanish settlers cruelly. He also forced the Indians to give up their gold, and sent many of them to Spain as slaves. On his third voyage in 1498 he was arrested and sent home to Spain in chains.

Queen Isabella gave him one more chance, sending him on a fourth voyage in 1502 to look for a strait that might connect the Caribbean

Sea to the Pacific Ocean. The expedition was a disaster: his ships became unseaworthy with marine worms, and Columbus had to be rescued from Jamaica. He returned to Spain a broken, bitter man.

Right The 'Cathedral Primada de America' in Santo Domingo was completed in 1540. More than 300 years later, Columbus's remains were interred there.

CLAIMING THE NEW WORLD

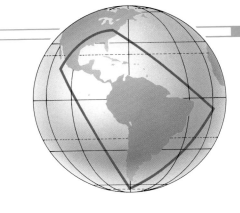

Before Columbus's death in 1506, Spain had established a major colony on Hispaniola, and both the Spanish and the Portuguese had begun to explore the coasts of Central and South America in search of gold and new territories to colonize.

To prevent unnecessary squabbles, in 1494 Spain and Portugal signed the Treaty of Tordesillas. A line was drawn down the world at 370 leagues (about 2 000 kilometres/1 250 miles) to the west of the Cape Verde Islands. Any newly discovered territories to the west of the line would be Spanish, and any to the east would be Portuguese.

Brazil was discovered by accident by the Portuguese navigator Pedro Álvares Cabral in 1500. He named the area he discovered 'Land of the True Cross'. Since it was to the east of the line of Tordesillas, Portugal could claim it. The remainder of South America was later claimed by Spain.

There was little attempt to explore the interior of the new continent for the time being. In 1513, however, Vasco Núñez de Balboa crossed the isthmus of Central America in Panama and became the first European to see the Pacific Ocean, which he promptly claimed for Spain.

Left Navigational tools remained simple throughout this period. Windroses such as this helped navigators to plot the course of their ship by recording the direction, strength and frequency of the wind.

Below Fernandez de Córdoba reached the Yucatán peninsula in 1517, and became the first European to see remains of the Mayan civilization, such as the spectacular pyramid at Tikal in Guatemala. He was followed by Juan de Grijalva in 1518, who was the first European to learn of the Aztecs.

Left The early explorers came across all kinds of animals and plants which were new to them. Artists attempting to illustrate their tales back at home often misunderstood what was being described to them, which is why these flying fish appear to be soaring like birds among the ship's rigging.

Fruits of exploration

A number of plants and foods that are familiar to us today were seen by Europeans for the first time in the Caribbean. Columbus was the first to report on the pineapple. Potato, maize and tobacco are all originally Taino (Arawak) words. The Arawaks used to smoke rolled-up tobacco leaves through their nostrils, much to the alarm and amusement of the explorers and the disbelief of those they told this to on their return to Europe.

European sailors slept on the deck before they discovered the comfortable hanging beds which the Arawaks called hammocks. Other words in the English language which probably come from the Taino language include canoe, cannibal, hurricane and barbecue.

Right Cabral, Vespucci and others began to acquire an understanding of the scale of the landmass of South America. The exploration of the Americas, however, was to follow from the voyages of Balboa and Córdoba.

The United States of Americus!

Amerigo Vespucci (1454–1512) was an Italian from Florence who was posted to Spain as an agent for a bank. He took a keen interest in exploration and supported Columbus on his first voyage. In 1499 he joined an expedition which explored the mouth of the Amazon, and in 1501–1502 he sailed down much of the east coast of South America. Unlike Columbus, he was convinced that this coast was not part of the Far East, but belonged to a continent he called the New World.

In 1508, Vespucci was appointed Pilot Major (examiner of ships' pilots) — a position he held till he died in 1512.

When Martin Waldseemüller, the noted geographer, produced a new map of the world in 1507, he proposed that this new continent should be called America, after Vespucci's Latinized name, Americus Vespuccius.

However, by 1513 Waldseemüller felt that Vespucci's contribution had not been so great after all. Too late: the name America had been accepted.

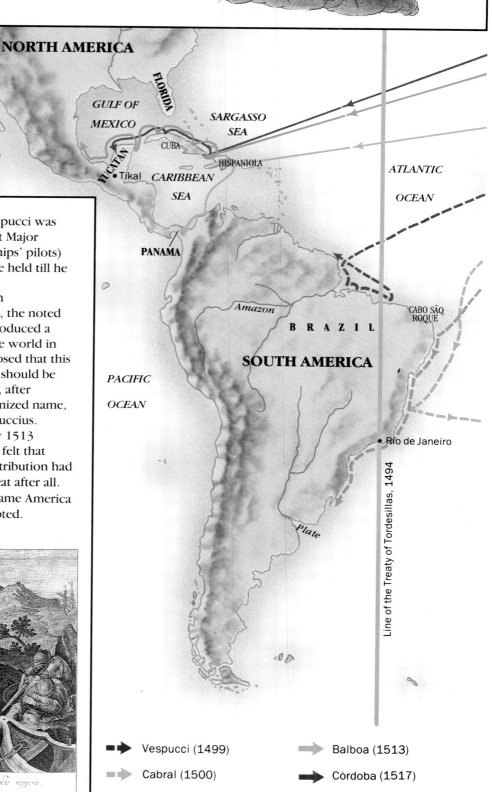

NORTH AMERICA

FLORIDA

GULF OF MEXICO

SARGASSO SEA

CUBA

YUCATAN

• Tikal CARIBBEAN SEA

HISPANIOLA

ATLANTIC OCEAN

PANAMA

Amazon

B R A Z I L

CABO SÃO ROQUE

SOUTH AMERICA

PACIFIC OCEAN

• Río de Janeiro

Line of the Treaty of Tordesillas, 1494

Plate

➡ Vespucci (1499)	➡ Balboa (1513)
➡ Cabral (1500)	➡ Córdoba (1517)
➡ Vespucci (1501-02)	➡ Grijalva (1518)

CIRCUMNAVIGATION

In the first two decades of the 16th century the Spanish had seen the 'Southern Ocean' (the Pacific) from Central America, and the Portuguese had seen it from South-East Asia (see pages 30–31). What lay between these two points was a mystery which many explorers were keen to solve.

The big question was still whether there was a sea-route to the East across or around the Americas. This was particularly important to Spain. If the route could be found, Spain might be able to reach and claim some of the Spice Islands under the Treaty of Tordesillas (see pages 58–59).

In 1519 Ferdinand Magellan, a Portuguese captain working for Spain, was sent to find out. He found a passage around the southern tip of South America. He named the sea beyond this the Pacific ('peaceful') Ocean because it was so calm.

Magellan was killed in the Philippines, and by this time the Spice Islands had been claimed by the Portuguese. But all was not lost: Magellan's expedition could claim to be the first ever to sail round (or circumnavigate) the world.

It was over 50 years before this feat was repeated, by Francis Drake.

Half the way round

Ferdinand Magellan (about 1480–1521) was an experienced navigator who had accompanied Afonso de Albuquerque's expedition to South-East Asia in 1511 (see pages 30–31). When the king of Portugal refused to send him on further expeditions, he turned to the king of Spain. He proposed to find a route that would allow Spain to reach the Spice Islands by sailing from east to west. In 1519 he set off for South America with five ships and a crew of 241 men. In 1520 his ships sailed through the strait at the tip of South America (above) now called after him. Half way round the world, there was a skirmish on the island of Mactan and Magellan was killed.

The surviving members of the expedition continued under the captaincy of Juan Sebastián del Cano. In the end only one ship, the *Victoria*, reached Spain in 1522. On board were 18 of the men who had sailed from Spain in 1519.

AMERICAE SIVE NOVI ORBIS, NOVA DESCRIPTIO.

Left This map of 1578 shows Tierra del Fuego attached to an unknown southern continent *terra incognita*, based on Magellan's observations. It was Drake's expedition of 1577–1580 that established that Tierra del Fuego is an island by sailing to its south, through what is now known as Drake Passage. Drake sailed up the Pacific coast of South America to plunder Spanish settlements there. By the time he reached England his holds were laden with silver, gold, spices and porcelain, which he presented to Queen Elizabeth I, who promptly knighted him.

'The Dragon'

The English captain Francis Drake (about 1540–1596) was a brilliant navigator, but to the Spanish he was little more than a pirate. After the repeated success of his raids against Spanish settlements in the Caribbean and Central America, they called him 'El Draco', the Dragon.

In 1577 Drake, with the approval of Queen Elizabeth I, set off on a voyage of exploration to the southern seas. By the time he reached the Pacific Ocean three of his ships had been lost, and one had returned to England, but Drake continued on the *Golden Hind* (right) and raided Valparaíso and Lima. Searching for a strait that would lead back to the Atlantic, he landed in northern California, which he named New Albion and claimed for England. He then headed westwards and completed his circumnavigation in 1580.

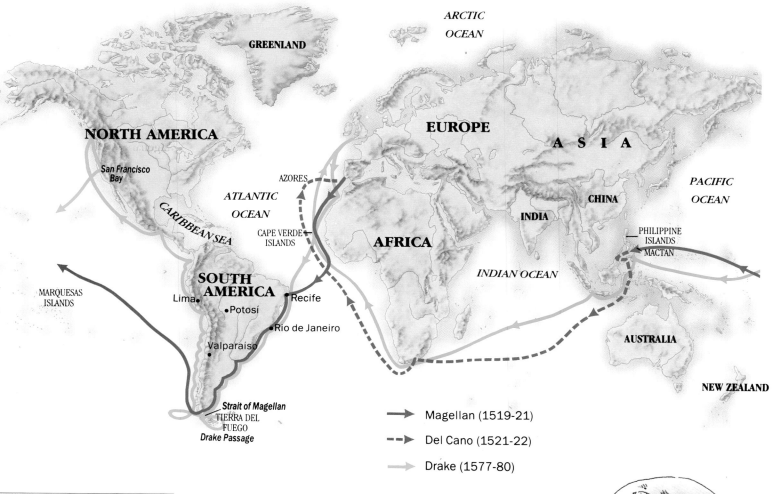

→ Magellan (1519-21)

--→ Del Cano (1521-22)

→ Drake (1577-80)

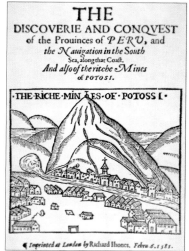

Above Both Magellan's and Drake's expeditions followed more or less the same course. Magellan's expedition came close to disaster when becalmed in the south-east Pacific. Drake avoided the region by sailing up the west coast of the Americas.

Left The town of Potosí, in southern Bolivia, was founded by the Spanish in 1546 around a rich silver mine. In 1579 Drake attacked and plundered a ship loaded with Potosí silver.

Survival rations

One of the survivors of Magellan's expedition was the Italian Antonio Pigafetta. He wrote a famous account of the journey, in which he described some of the terrible hardships endured by the crew. They came close to starvation in the eastern Pacific, and only survived by eating sawdust, leather and rotting biscuits such as this, which were often contaminated by rats' droppings, and by drinking foul water.

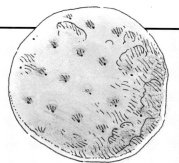

THE CONQUISTADORS

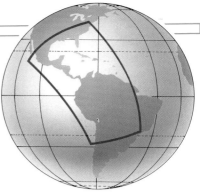

In 1519 Hernán Cortés (1485–1547) was appointed by the Spanish governor of Cuba to lead an expedition to 'New Spain' (Mexico), which Juan de Grijalva had visited the year before. Cortés was a 'conquistador', a warrior in pursuit of conquest in the name of Spain and Christianity.

He landed in New Spain with only 600 men, but he quickly made alliances with various Indian peoples, such as the Totonacs and Tlaxcaltecs, who did not like being ruled by the Aztecs. At Tenochtitlán, the Aztec capital, they found the Aztecs in a state of confusion, and Cortés succeeded in taking hostage their leader, Montezuma. After a series of bitter squabbles and battles, the Spanish and their Indian allies laid siege to Tenochtitlán and in 1521 the Aztecs were defeated. Within five years Cortés had control of the whole of the Aztec Empire.

Cortés was never appointed viceroy of Mexico as he had hoped. He was created Marquis del Valle de Oaxaca. After his death in Spain, his remains were returned to Mexico.

Cortés' daring conquest set the tone for the next great feat of the conquistadors: the conquest of Peru in 1532 by Francisco Pizarro.

South America was changed for ever — by conquest, and also by European diseases. The population of South America in 1519 has been estimated at 57 million; in 1607 it was 4 million.

Above Hernán Cortés brought a new level of ruthlessness to the Spanish conquest of the Americas which caused offence in Spain even in his own day. He died in Spain in 1547, resentful that his achievements had not been properly acknowledged.

Below A group of monumental cities such as this , Teotihuacán, surrounded the Aztec capital Tenochtitlán. It was at Tenochtitlán that Cortés finally forced the Aztecs to submit to Spanish rule when Cuauhtemac surrendered the city to the Spanish conquistador. He went on to conquer Honduras and his armies took control of Guatemala and El Salvador.

The Mendoza Codex

The Aztecs compiled books written in pictures, called *codices*, which tell us what life was like in Aztec times. In the 16th century, when the Spanish were firmly in control of Mexico, the governor, Antonio de Mendoza, ordered a codex to be made for the king of Spain to show him what life was like in Mexico at the time. This is one of the pages from the Mendoza Codex.

In the name of God

Francisco Pizarro (1476–1541) had heard rumours of the gold of the Incas in 1513, when he accompanied Balboa's expedition across Central America (see pages 58–59). After Cortés' conquest of the Aztecs, Pizarro became determined to conquer the Incas.

His first attempts in 1524 and 1526 failed, but in 1532 he reached Peru with just 185 men and 27 horses. They found the Inca Empire

Eldorado

The Spanish found vast quantities of gold such as this mask in South America, particularly in Colombia and Peru. Many conquistadors were inspired to press further into unexplored regions by the legend of the Golden Man, 'El Dorado' the ruler of a land of gold. The possible location of the land of Eldorado moved as each region was explored, and it was never found.

Below The conquistadors destroyed the great empires of Central and South America with extraordinarily small forces. The Spanish had several important advantages: they had gunpowder and firearms, armour and horses, all of which terrified their opposition, who had none of these.

Below Both Cortés and Pizarro travelled fairly short distances to reach the heart of civilizations previously unknown to them. Their expeditions could be described as conquest rather than exploration.

GULF OF MEXICO

BAHAMAS

CUBA

Tenochtitlán (Mexico City)

Veracruz

YUCATÁN

GULF OF HONDURAS

HISPANIOLA

JAMAICA

CARIBBEAN SEA

Panama

Quito

SOUTH AMERICA

Marañon

Tangaiaia

Cajamarca

Ucayali

Santa

Lima

Machu Picchu

Cuzco

Lake Titicaca

Andes Mountains

→ Cortés (1519)

→ Pizarro (1531-32)

→ Pizarro (1533)

on the verge of civil war, as two princes, Atahualpa and Huáscar, contested the throne. Pizarro exploited this situation. He invited Atahualpa to a meeting in Cajamarca. But it was a trick: when Atahualpa rejected the offer of becoming Christian the Spanish massacred the Incas and captured Atahualpa.

To win his freedom, the Incas had to fill a large room with gold and silver. But meanwhile Atahualpa managed to arrange the assassination of Huáscar.

Atahualpa was tried by the Spanish and executed for murder. The Inca Empire fell into chaos, and Pizarro was able to march into its capital, Cuzco. However, the Spanish then squabbled among themselves, and Pizarro himself was murdered by rivals in 1541.

Right Machu Picchu, an Inca fortress and settlement high up in the Andes, lay forgotten for centuries until it was rediscovered in 1911.

SCIENTIFIC EXPLORATION

Several of the Spanish conquistadors in the 16th and early 17th century took the search for Eldorado over the Andes and into the interior of South America. In 1542 Francisco de Orellana travelled down much of the Amazon. An encounter with one tribe reminded him of the women warriors called Amazons in Ancient Greek legend — so the river gained its name.

The huge advances in science over the next two centuries, however, brought a new kind of explorer to South America: the scientist in search of knowledge. One of the greatest of these was the German geologist and naturalist Baron Alexander von Humboldt. From 1799–1804 he explored much of the Orinoco River, then he travelled through the northern Andes to Peru. His painstaking methods of research set the standard for all scientific expeditions that followed including the one that was to have the most profound effect on people's understanding of their own evolution.

From 1831–1836 the British naturalist Charles Darwin sailed around the coasts of South America on board HMS *Beagle* — a voyage that was to result in a radical change in the way people understood the world.

Three British scientists, Alfred Russell Wallace, Henry Bates and Richard Spruce, spent a combined total of 32 years in the Amazon region from 1848 on, and collected thousands of specimens of plants, insects and other animals. They suffered from malaria and dysentery, and faced constant danger from turbulent rivers, alligators and snakes — all in the cause of science.

Below The Galápagos Islands lie on the Equator, 1 100 km (680 miles) to the west of South America. Ecuador took possession of them in 1832, three years before the *Beagle* anchored in their waters.

Scientist and hero

Alexander von Humboldt (1769–1859) was an energetic scientist who made observations about everything he came upon — geology, geography, climate, botany, people. He travelled with a large set of scientific instruments, collected thousands of specimens and made detailed notes. His sketches formed the basis for the illustrations, such as this balsa raft on the Orinoco River, used in popular accounts of his journeys.

In South America he was accompanied by the French doctor Aimé Bonpland (1773–1858). They carried out numerous experiments, often at great risk to themselves. During an earthquake, for example, Humboldt calmly set about measuring the electricity in the atmosphere. In just five years they travelled about 64 000 km (40 000 miles), and returned home with 335 cases of specimens.

Back in Europe Humboldt was treated as a hero and was honoured by many institutions. He devoted his last years to writing.

Descended from the apes

Charles Darwin (1809–1882) was only 22 years old when he joined HMS *Beagle* (left) for its five-year voyage around South America. It took him a further 23 years to produce the book which explained his new theory of evolution. *On the Origin of Species by Means of Natural Selection* was published in 1859. Darwin's ideas were considered revolutionary at the time. They appeared to contradict the Bible, which said the world had been created by God in six days. In his book *The Descent of Man*, published in 1871, he took the idea one step further by suggesting that the human species was descended from apes.

Despite the alarm these new ideas caused, Darwin was celebrated as a major figure of his day, and many of his ideas were quickly adopted.

Right Humboldt and Darwin, as well as scientists working in the Amazon Basin, revealed the immense riches of South America, but they covered only a small part of its vast area. Despite increasing amounts of land being taken over for farming and ranching, large areas still remain virtually unexplored today.

→ Humboldt and Bonpland (1799-1800)
⇢ Humboldt and Bonpland (1801-1803)
→ Darwin (1831-35)

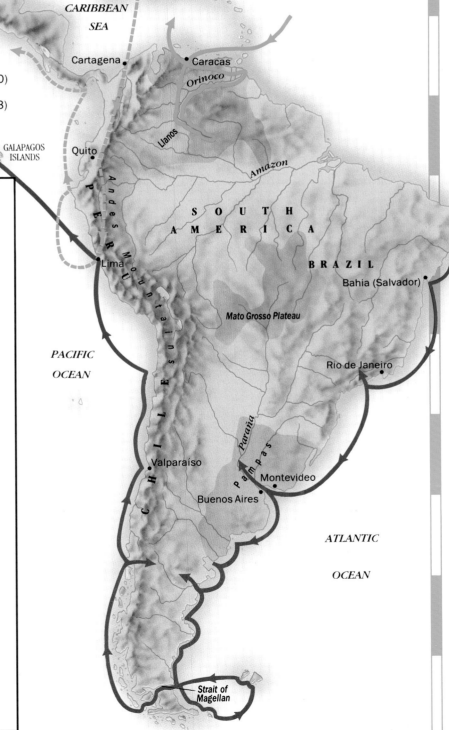

CARIBBEAN SEA

Cartagena
Caracas
Orinoco
Quito
Llanos
Amazon
GALAPAGOS ISLANDS
Andes Mountains
PERU
Lima
SOUTH AMERICA
BRAZIL
Bahia (Salvador)
Mato Grosso Plateau
PACIFIC OCEAN
Rio de Janeiro
CHILE
Paraná
Pampas
Valparaíso
Montevideo
Buenos Aires
ATLANTIC OCEAN
Strait of Magellan

A world of its own

Darwin noticed that the wildlife on the Galápagos Islands had adapted over many generations to the special conditions on the islands. For instance, finches such as the ones above had evolved different-shaped beaks according to whether they ate nuts, insects or fruit. Colonies of giant tortoises, living in isolation on various islands, had developed in different ways. (*Galápago* means tortoise in Spanish.)

Such observations helped Darwin to form his ideas on evolution based on what he called 'natural selection'. The animals that survive are the ones that have the features that are best suited to their environment. They are the most likely to breed successfully and these features will be passed on.

EASTERN NORTH AMERICA

The east coast of North America had been visited by Vikings in around AD 1000 (see pages 16–17), but these experiences had been all but forgotten by the 15th century. When the Italian navigator John Cabot sailed from Bristol, England, in 1497 and reached Newfoundland, he thought that it was China.

The search then began for the Northwest Passage — a route to the East around the north coast of Canada. This led the French navigator Jacques Cartier up the St Lawrence River in 1534. Martin Frobisher made several efforts to find the Northwest Passage from 1576 to 1578; likewise John Davis in 1585–1587, Henry Hudson in 1609–1611, William Baffin and Robert Bylot in 1615 and 1616 — all of them failed to find the Passage and many began to wonder if it existed at all.

The search for the Northwest Passage overshadowed the opportunities offered by North America itself. Several attempts were made to set up colonies, by the Portuguese in the 1520s, the French and Spanish in the 1560s, and the English in the 1580s and 1590s, but little came of them.

In 1603, however, the French explorer Samuel de Champlain (1567–1635) travelled up the St Lawrence River looking for land to settle. He founded Quebec in 1608, and both Dutch and English settlements along the east coast followed soon after.

Below Frobisher met the Inuit on his first voyage of 1576. Although contact with them was initially friendly, the Inuit abducted five of his crew. Frobisher responded by seizing an Inuit couple.

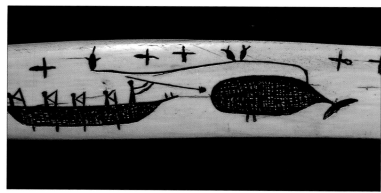

From east to west

French and British fur traders and trappers were responsible for much of the exploration of the continent during the 17th and 18th centuries. Alexander Mackenzie (about 1764–1820) was a Scottish fur trader who worked for the North West Company. Mackenzie was interested in opening up a route that would lead across Canada to the Pacific. In 1789, accompanied by an Indian chief and several French Canadians with their Indian wives, he followed a river from Lake Athabasca. Unfortunately this led north-west to flow into the Arctic Ocean. The river is now named after him.

In 1792–1793 he led a similar party along the Peace River then down part of the Fraser River to reach the Pacific and become the first recorded European to cross North America north of Mexico.

Above The Inuit, or Eskimos, were found right across the northern coast of Canada, as well as in Alaska and Siberia. Living by hunting and trapping, they offered valuable trade in furs and walrus ivory. Some early explorers in search of the Northwest Passage thought that the Asian features of the Inuit meant that China was not far off. The Inuit were also skilled whalers, as we can see from this carving on a walrus ivory show knife of the 19th century.

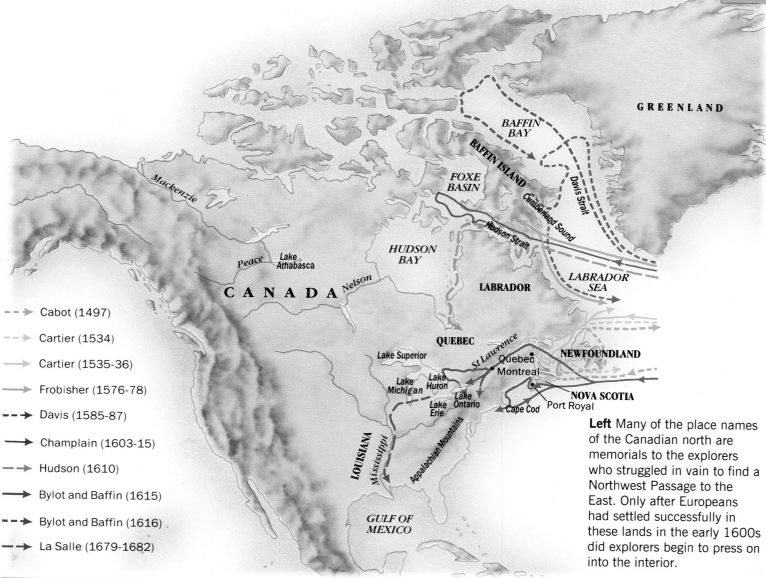

- - -➤ Cabot (1497)
- - -➤ Cartier (1534)
——➤ Cartier (1535-36)
——➤ Frobisher (1576-78)
- - -➤ Davis (1585-87)
——➤ Champlain (1603-15)
- - ➤ Hudson (1610)
——➤ Bylot and Baffin (1615)
- - ➤ Bylot and Baffin (1616)
— - ➤ La Salle (1679-1682)

Left Many of the place names of the Canadian north are memorials to the explorers who struggled in vain to find a Northwest Passage to the East. Only after Europeans had settled successfully in these lands in the early 1600s did explorers begin to press on into the interior.

Louisiana

In 1679 the French explorer Robert de La Salle (1643–1687) set off from the Great Lakes to pioneer a trade route southwards across the heart of North America. He travelled down the Mississippi River to the Gulf of Mexico, setting up trading forts along the way. He declared the vast territory he had covered to be French and called it Louisiana, in honour of his king, Louis XIV.

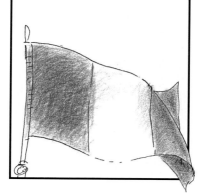

Abandoned at sea

Henry Hudson made three journeys to the northern seas in search of a passage to the East. In 1609, sailing for the Dutch East India Company, he explored much of the east coast of North America. In 1610, sponsored by English merchants, he reached Hudson Bay. Forced to spend a gruelling winter there, his crew mutinied and put him in a boat with his son and loyal members of the crew. They were never seen again. Hudson's name is recalled in the bay, in the Hudson River and Mountains, in the two towns named after him, and in the Hudson Bay Company which did much to open up huge areas of North America.

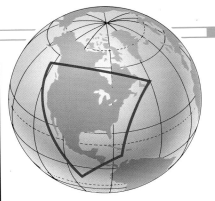

WESTERN NORTH AMERICA

Once established in the Caribbean and Central America, the Spanish conquistadors spread out in all directions, including northwards into North America.

The navigator Juan Ponce de Léon visited the coast of Florida in 1513. Spanish expeditions later pushed northwards from Mexico by land and sea, still in search of Eldorado (see pages 62–63). Francisco Vásquez de Coronado reached as far north as modern Kansas in 1540–1542, while his colleague Garcia Lopez de Cárdenas reached the Grand Canyon in modern Arizona, in the west of the continent.

Meanwhile others explored the west coast. Francisco de Ulloa explored the Gulf of California in 1539–1540; Juan Rodríguez Cabrillo reached the site of modern San Francisco in 1543.

In the late 18th century the west coast of Canada was surveyed by several scientific expeditions, including those of Bruno de Heceta and Juan de la Bodega y Cuadra in 1775, and Alessandro Malaspina in 1791–1792. George Vancouver who sailed with Captain Cook on his second and third voyages, was in the region at the same time, and claimed it for Britain.

By the end of the 18th century the east-coast American states were pressing westwards. The 19th century saw a concerted effort by the United States to map the West, which coincided with white settlement and increasingly bitter conflict with the Indians.

The Louisiana Purchase

In 1803, the United States government purchased Louisiana — a huge tract of French territory in central North America. President Jefferson asked Meriwether Lewis, seen here in typical frontiersman garb, to lead a 'Corps of Discovery' across the land to the Pacific — a journey that took almost 18 months to complete.

Above The Rocky Mountains, rising to over 4 000 m (13 000 ft), form a natural barrier between the Great Plains of North America and the west coast. Until Lewis crossed them, the Rockies were known only to fur trappers — often French Canadians.

Above Spanish settlements in North America were pioneered by Juan de Oñate in 1598, and a Catholic mission was founded in Santa Fe in 1609. Others followed, spreading across the south-west.

Left The first white men to see the spectacular Grand Canyon were members of an expedition led by Garcia Lopez de Cárdenas in 1540. It was explored in 1776, by James O. Peattie, a fur trapper.

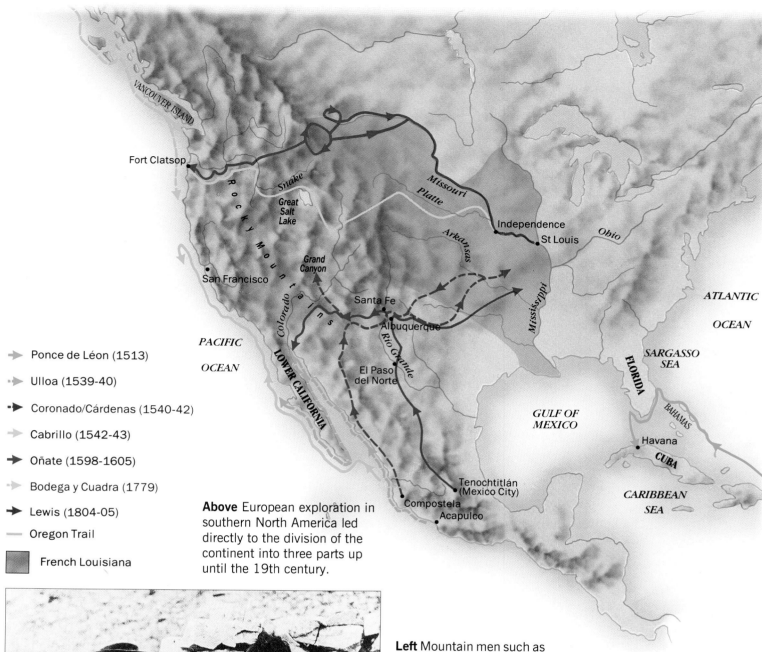

- ➤ Ponce de Léon (1513)
- ➤ Ulloa (1539-40)
- ➤ Coronado/Cárdenas (1540-42)
- ➤ Cabrillo (1542-43)
- ➤ Oñate (1598-1605)
- ➤ Bodega y Cuadra (1779)
- ➤ Lewis (1804-05)
- — Oregon Trail
- ▨ French Louisiana

Above European exploration in southern North America led directly to the division of the continent into three parts up until the 19th century.

Left Mountain men such as John Moss, seen here with the Paiute Indian chief Tercherum, played an important part in opening up the West. The US army used their specialized knowledge and friendships with local Indians as they were posted westward to protect settlers, especially those who followed the Oregon Trail.

Below Trading posts such as Fort Laramie offered welcome protection from marauding Indians to wagon trains. These carried settlers and their families who came in ever-increasing numbers, hoping to make their fortunes in the new lands of the American West.

The Aborigines of Australia and the islanders of the South Pacific lived in comparative isolation for many thousands of years until the European explorers arrived.

THE FIRST SETTLERS

The Aborigines of Australia reached their continent some 50 000 years ago, probably by island-hopping from South-East Asia, then walking from New Guinea when the sea level was lower than it is today. About 10 000 years ago the first occupants of the islands of the South Pacific sailed forth, also from South-East Asia, to Melanesia. Polynesia was settled about 3 500 years ago, and Micronesia about 3 000 years ago. The Polynesians then spread out to reach New Zealand in about AD 950.

The skills of the Polynesian navigators allowed them to sail for many days out of sight of land, judging their position by the stars, the swell, and the flight of sea birds. Similarly, the Aborigines knew their huge and often difficult terrain intimately. Routes called songlines led right across the continent.

These societies had little to offer the rest of the world in terms of trade or gold. But they did have land, and this began to be taken from them by the Europeans in the 18th century.

Ownership of the land is still a matter of contention in both countries, and many Maoris in New Zealand consider the British failed to honour treaty obligations.

Dreamtime

The Aborigines of Australia believe that the world was created during Dreamtime, when giant animals with human characters shaped the world out of a grey, flat mass. The Aboriginal way of life and their code of behaviour was also set out during Dreamtime and handed down through the generations. Most Aboriginal works of art such as the intricately patterned bark-painting (right) relate to Dreamtime. The man below is making a didgeridoo, a traditional wind instrument, the origins of which are lost in the mists of time. Aboriginal art and culture is much studied today by anthropologists.

Left There are tens of thousands of islands such as Tahiti in the South Pacific, mostly lying within the Tropics.

Below The South Pacific islands were occupied by settlers, originally from South-East Asia, who arrived over a period of 10 000 years or more. For their part, the Aborigines of Australia had occupied their land for 50 000 years before European arrival.

They couldn't believe their eyes!

Much of the wildlife of Australia is unique. All but a few obscure marsupials (animals with pouches) come from this region, including the kangaroo, koala and wombat. The egg-laying duck-billed platypus is so unusual that, when first shown a skin in 1797, scientists thought it was a hoax.

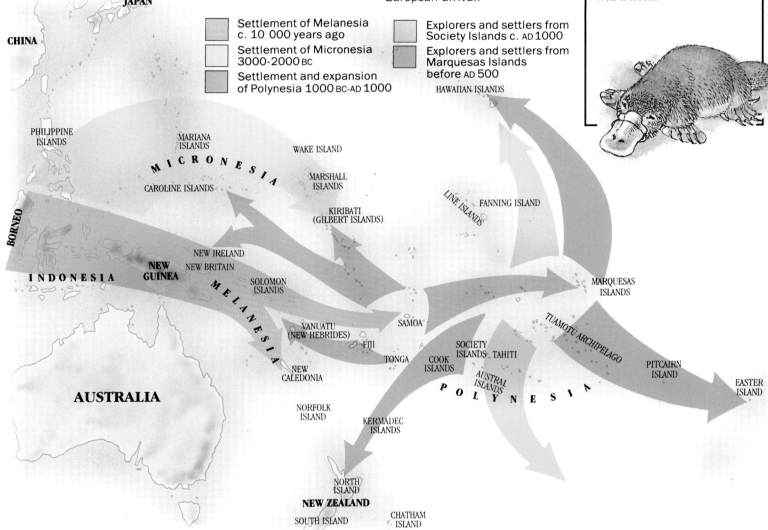

Settlement of Melanesia c. 10 000 years ago

Settlement of Micronesia 3000-2000 BC

Settlement and expansion of Polynesia 1000 BC-AD 1000

Explorers and settlers from Society Islands c. AD 1000

Explorers and settlers from Marquesas Islands before AD 500

JAPAN

CHINA

HAWAIIAN ISLANDS

PHILIPPINE ISLANDS

MARIANA ISLANDS

WAKE ISLAND

M I C R O N E S I A

CAROLINE ISLANDS

MARSHALL ISLANDS

LINE ISLANDS

FANNING ISLAND

KIRIBATI (GILBERT ISLANDS)

BORNEO

NEW IRELAND

NEW BRITAIN

NEW GUINEA

INDONESIA

SOLOMON ISLANDS

M E L A N E S I A

MARQUESAS ISLANDS

VANUATU (NEW HEBRIDES)

SAMOA

FIJI

TUAMOTU ARCHIPELAGO

TONGA

COOK ISLANDS

SOCIETY ISLANDS

TAHITI

PITCAIRN ISLAND

EASTER ISLAND

NEW CALEDONIA

AUSTRAL ISLANDS

P O L Y N E S I A

AUSTRALIA

NORFOLK ISLAND

KERMADEC ISLANDS

NORTH ISLAND

NEW ZEALAND

SOUTH ISLAND

CHATHAM ISLAND

Maori culture

The Polynesians first settled in New Zealand (right) about 1 000 years ago. They called this land Aotearoa, and developed their own distinctive Maori culture, living by fishing and farming. They wore cloaks made of feathers, and the chieftains tatooed their faces with complex spiralling patterns.

TERRA INCOGNITA AUSTRALIS

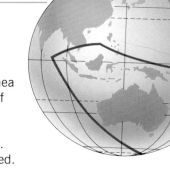

By the 1530s, European explorers had travelled to Africa, South America and the Far East, but a major mystery still intrigued them. Where was the great southern continent shown on Ptolemy's map (see pages 10–11) and known as *Terra Australis*, 'southern land'?

The Spanish conquistadors, believing Inca legends, hoped that such lands might contain rich new sources of gold as well as new territories to claim. They sent a number of expeditions to the South Pacific from the 1530s onwards. In 1606 Fernandez de Quiros set out from Peru and found a new land which he named La Austrialia del Espiritu Santo, but it was an island of the New Hebrides (Vanuatu).

That same year the Dutchman Willem Jansz became the first recorded European to set eyes on Australia. He sailed into the Gulf of Carpentaria to make the first known European landing in Australia. The reconnaissance that followed culminated in the voyages of Abel Tasman. The Dutch were now the new power in the Southern Seas and had soon built a trading empire for themselves based on Batavia (Jakarta), founded in 1619.

Australia was named New Holland by the

Below People of Papua New Guinea. The name New Guinea reflected European dreams of finding gold in the South Pacific, just as it had been found in Guinea, West Africa. Such hopes were disappointed.

Dutch. The north and west coasts became fairly familiar to them over the next few decades, and the systematic voyages of Abel Tasman in the 1640s began to reveal the shape of these new lands. But trading opportunities seemed slim, and so the Dutch showed little interest in pursuing their discoveries.

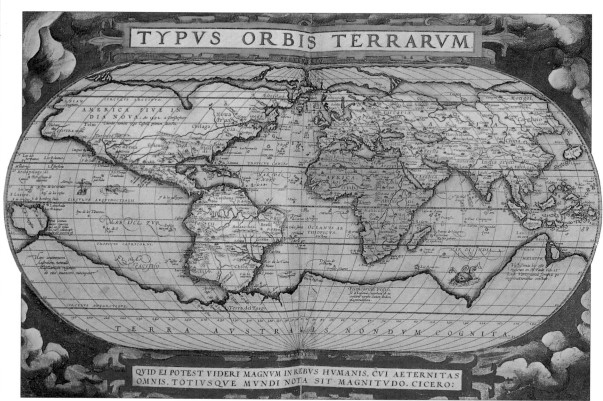

TYPVS ORBIS TERRARVM

QVID EI POTEST VIDERI MAGNVM IN REBVS HVMANIS, CVI AETERNITAS OMNIS, TOTIVSQVE MVNDI NOTA SIT MAGNITVDO. CICERO:

Left This map of 1570 shows a huge southern continent attached to Tierra del Fuego, off the southern coast of South America. Here it is called *Terra Australis Nondum Cognita*, 'southern land not yet discovered'. Only the vague shape of northern Australia appears, based on reports by Portuguese navigators who followed in Magellan's wake after he had made the first crossing of the Pacific in 1520–1521.

The Dutch East Indies

The Dutch adventure in South-East Asia began in 1595 when Cornelis de Houtman sailed from the Netherlands to the South Seas with 249 men. Only 89 men returned, but their journey took them to the islands of Indonesia, including Java and Bali. Reports of these rich lands caused excitement in Amsterdam.

In 1602 the *Verenigde Oostindische Compagnie* (*VOC* — United East India Company) was formed and it soon took over most of the Portuguese trade in Indonesia. It became the world's most powerful trading organisation.

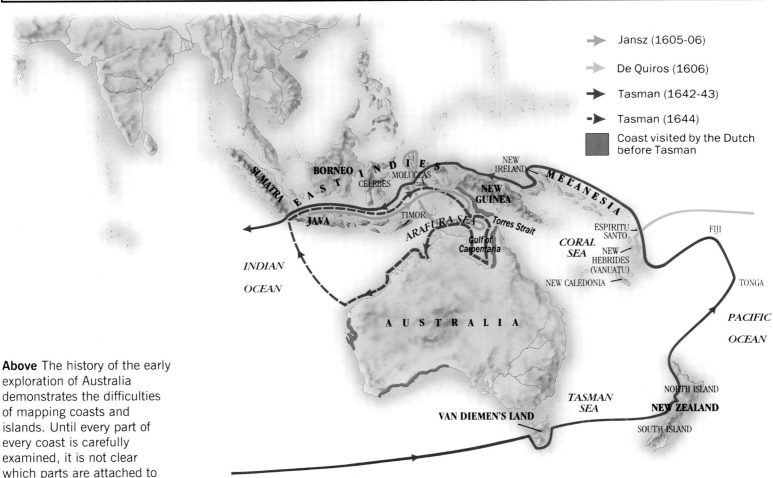

→ Jansz (1605-06)

→ De Quiros (1606)

→ Tasman (1642-43)

⇢ Tasman (1644)

⬛ Coast visited by the Dutch before Tasman

Above The history of the early exploration of Australia demonstrates the difficulties of mapping coasts and islands. Until every part of every coast is carefully examined, it is not clear which parts are attached to which others.

Dutch Australasia

Abel Jansz Tasman (1603–1659) entered the service of the Dutch East India Company in 1632, and spent most of the rest of his life in the Far East. He led two major expeditions, in 1642 and 1644. The 1642 voyage proved that 'New Holland' (Australia) was an island. It also made Tasman the first European to visit Aotearoa, which he renamed New Zealand. (Zeeland is a province of the Netherlands.)

Tasman's voyages made a major contribution to European knowledge of the region. His map of 1644, however, shows that his expedition of that year failed to grasp that New Guinea was a separate island. Also, Van Diemen's Land (Tasmania — right) is shown on his map as part of mainland Australia.

CAPTAIN COOK

Over a century passed, and the huge territories visited by Abel Tasman in the 1640s remained virtually blank and unclaimed on the map even though much of the rest of the South Pacific was now being claimed by several European nations.

In 1768 James Cook (1728–1779) was appointed leader of a British naval expedition to the South Pacific to observe the passage of Venus between the Earth and the Sun. Cook, the son of a Yorkshire farm labourer, had risen rapidly through the naval ranks and was one of the first explorers to travel in the interests of knowledge and science. But he was also given secret instructions to locate *Terra Australis* once and for all, and to claim it for Great Britain. He sailed in the *Endeavour*, a coal ship specially fitted for surveying, and visited Tahiti, New Zealand and Australia.

Two further expeditions followed. During the second voyage (1772–1775) he circumnavigated the world close to the Antarctic Circle, and established that no habitable continent existed south of Australia. In the third voyage (1776–1780) he set out to see if there was a western entrance to the Northwest Passage. It proved to be his last, and he was killed in an incident on the Sandwich Islands (Hawaii).

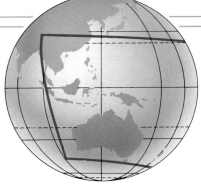

Left Cook was an exceptionally gifted navigator, a kind-hearted explorer, and a meticulous captain who cared deeply for the well-being of his crew.

Above Cook claimed Australia for Great Britain in April 1770 when he landed on an area of coast that now forms part of the suburbs of Sydney.

Below This world map was printed shortly after the return of Cook's last voyage.

The Limeys

One of the great killers on any long voyage in Cook's day was a disease called scurvy, caused by a lack of vitamin C. Victims would suffer from terrible sores, lose their teeth and waste away. Cook combated scurvy by insisting that his crew had as much fresh food as possible. In 1795 the British began to issue lime juice to their vessels which gave rise to the nickname 'limey' for British sailors.

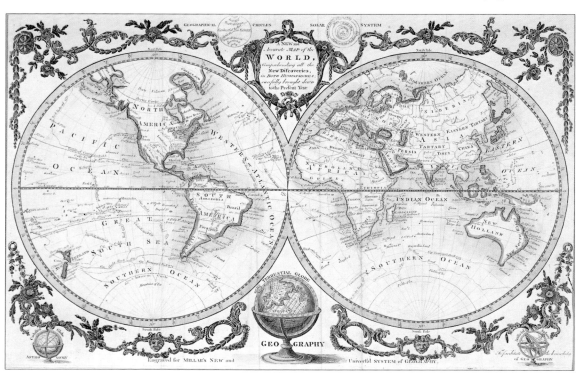

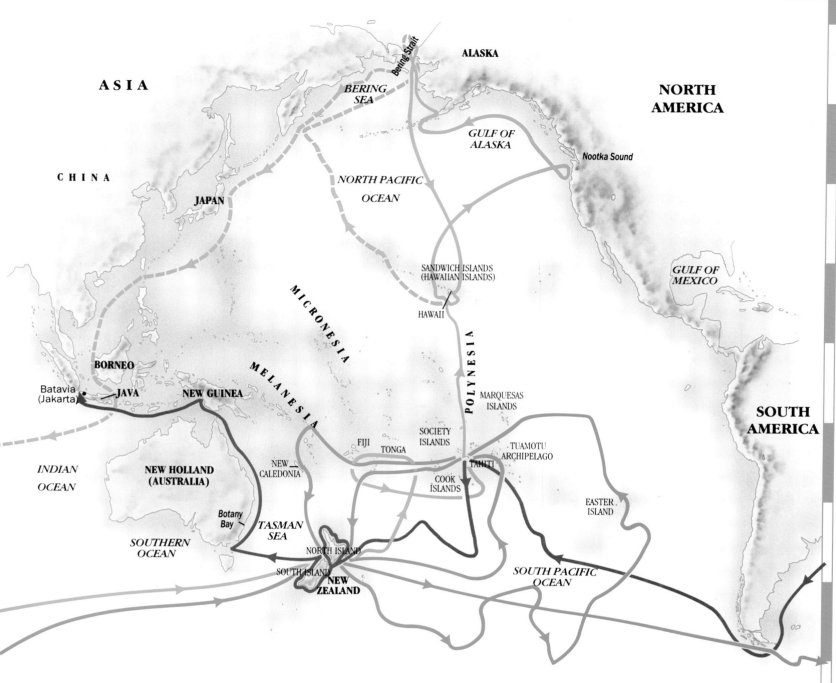

ALASKA

ASIA

BERING
SEA

NORTH
AMERICA

GULF OF
ALASKA

Bering Strait

CHINA

Nootka Sound

JAPAN

NORTH PACIFIC
OCEAN

GULF OF
MEXICO

SANDWICH ISLANDS
(HAWAIIAN ISLANDS)

M
I
C
R
O
N
E
S
I
A

HAWAII

P
O
L
Y
N
E
S
I
A

BORNEO

M
E
L
A
N
E
S
I
A

MARQUESAS
ISLANDS

SOUTH
AMERICA

Batavia
(Jakarta)

JAVA

NEW GUINEA

SOCIETY
ISLANDS

TUAMOTU
ARCHIPELAGO

FIJI

TONGA

TAHITI

INDIAN
OCEAN

NEW HOLLAND
(AUSTRALIA)

NEW
CALEDONIA

COOK
ISLANDS

EASTER
ISLAND

Botany
Bay

TASMAN
SEA

NORTH ISLAND

SOUTHERN
OCEAN

SOUTH ISLAND
NEW
ZEALAND

SOUTH PACIFIC
OCEAN

First expedition (1768-71)

Second expedition (1772-75)

Third expedition (1776-79)

Continuation of third expedition
after Cook's death (1779-80)

Above Cook's voyages
made the most thorough
examination of the Pacific up
until that time. With his skills
as a navigator, he fixed the
positions of many of the
islands for the first time.

Above Cook received a hostile
reception from the Maoris of
New Zealand when he first
reached their shores in 1769.
The highest mountain in New
Zealand still bears his name.

Right During Cook's third
voyage, a Sandwich islander
stole a boat, and Cook went to
investigate. The incident
turned into a violent dispute,
and Cook was killed.

75

CROSSING AUSTRALIA

The settlement of Australia began in 1788 with the arrival of the first shipment of convicts from Britain, sentenced to transportation instead of prison, and proceeded with the foundation of coastal cities such as Sydney, Adelaide, Melbourne and, in the west, Perth.

Matthew Flinders and George Bass had conducted extensive surveys of all the coasts by 1802, but the interior of Australia remained a mystery to all but the Aborigines. Since rivers flowed inland from the coastal mountains, there was speculation that the middle of the continent might contain a vast sea, perhaps surrounded by fertile land. Charles Sturt failed to find this in his ventures inland from 1828 to 1846. Another explorer, Edward Eyre, had a similar disappointment in 1840 when he discovered only desert and salt flats.

Interest in the interior became more urgent with the coming of the telegraph and the need to lay long-distance cables. In 1859 the government of South Australia offered a prize to the first person to cross Australia south to north.

Robert O'Hara Burke and William Wills came tragically close to success in 1860–1861, but it was left to John McDouall Stuart to become the first to complete the journey the next year.

Above Those attempting to cross Australia from north to south had to travel over 2 000 km (1 250 miles) through rough terrain.

Above Burke and Wills were the first to see the merits of using imported camels in the interior of Australia. Camels later became widely used for carrying supplies and post to remote farms and settlements. Their drivers were referred to generally as 'Ghans', as many came from Afghanistan.

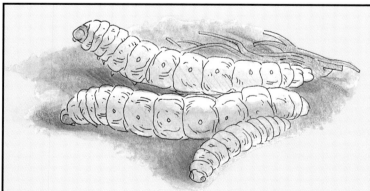

Good grub

Burke and Wills perished where Aborigines would have survived, and indeed it was Aborigines who kept their only surviving colleague, John King, alive. Aborigines have developed highly refined skills in hunting, knowing where water can be found, and using every possible form of food available. This includes a wide variety of wild fruits, seeds and roots, snakes and lizards, and insects and grubs, such as witchetty grubs (above). Their traditional medicine also comes from various wild plants and animals.

First there and back

The first expedition to cross Australia from north to south successfully was led by John McDouall Stuart (1815–1866). He had migrated to Australia from Scotland in 1839, and had accompanied Sturt on an expedition into the interior in 1844, before turning to professional surveying. (His sextant is pictured, right.) He began a series of journeys into the heart of Australia in 1859, reaching its centre in 1860, before making the complete crossing in 1861–1862.

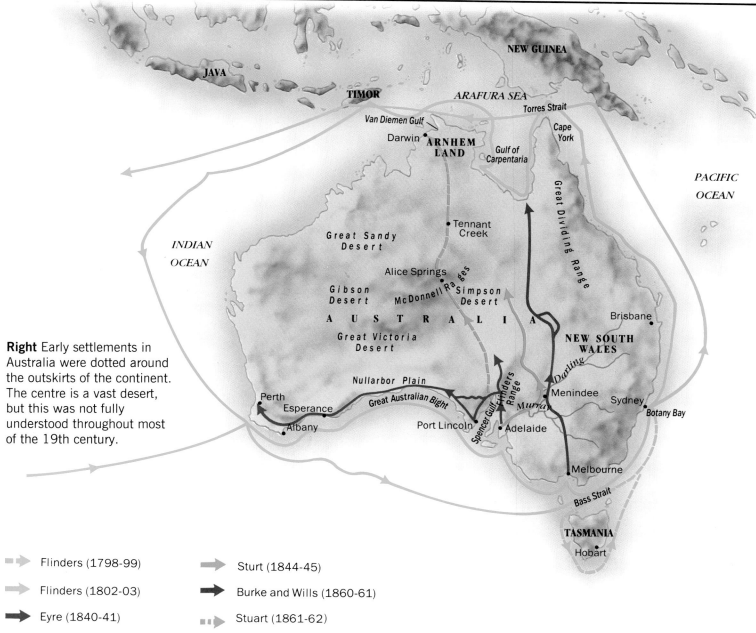

Right Early settlements in Australia were dotted around the outskirts of the continent. The centre is a vast desert, but this was not fully understood throughout most of the 19th century.

- ⇢ Flinders (1798-99)
- ⇢ Flinders (1802-03)
- ➡ Eyre (1840-41)
- ⇨ Sturt (1844-45)
- ➡ Burke and Wills (1860-61)
- ⇢ Stuart (1861-62)

Tragic failure

Burke (1820–1861) and Wills (1834–1861) set out from Melbourne in August 1860. Their expedition soon began to break up. Burke, Wills, Charles Gray and John King struck out alone from Cooper Creek, leaving William Brahe with the stores. Burke and Wills reached the Gulf of Carpentaria, then rejoined Gray and King for the journey home. Gray died before they stumbled into Cooper Creek seven hours after Brahe had left. By the time the second of two search parties (imaginatively portrayed in the popular press, far left) found them, only King was still alive.

NEW ZEALAND AND THE PACIFIC ISLANDS

Although Abel Tasman had visited Australia and New Zealand in the 1640s, the European powers were slow to investigate the South Pacific. Over time, however, enticing reports from these beautiful islands by passing adventurers began to fire the European imagination.

In the latter part of the 18th century governments started to sponsor voyages of scientific exploration, such as the British naval expedition to the Pacific under John ('Foulweather Jack') Byron in 1764. In 1767, sailing in the same ship, Samuel Wallis became the first European to visit Tahiti. Cook's famous voyages took place between 1768 and 1780 (see pages 74–75). But as elsewhere, exploration was followed by European claims to territory, especially from Britain and France who were both keen to expand their empires.

This same process was slowed down, but not halted, in New Zealand by the arrival of missionaries in 1814. They had considerable success in converting the Maoris to Christianity, and explored much of the land with Maoris as their guides. Defending Maori interests, the missionaries opposed the idea of European settlement, but in 1840 the first 1 000 settlers arrived and colonization began — eventually at the expense of the Maoris.

Above The Dutch admiral Jacob Roggeveen gave Easter Island its name because that was the day on which he reached it in 1722. Although it is set some distance from the main cluster of Polynesian islands, and 3 780 km (2 350 miles) from the South American coast, Polynesian settlers reached Easter Island in the distant past. About 1 000 years ago they carved over 600 enormous stone heads; some of them which still remain are as much as 20 m (65 ft) tall and weigh over 50 tonnes.

The real Robinson Crusoe

William Dampier (1650–1715) was one of a number of daring and ruthless English adventurers who roamed the Caribbean and the Pacific during the late 18th century. He made his fame and fortune by raiding Spanish settlements on the west coast of South America in 1679. He then travelled west to New Holland (Australia) before completing his trip around the world.

Dampier would be seen as just another buccaneer if he had not had a more thoughtful side. A keen observer of everything that presented itself to him, he wrote a colourful account of his voyage under the title *A New Voyage Round the World*. Published in 1697, it became a bestseller, helping to set alight the public's interest in the South Seas.

In 1699 he was selected to lead an official naval expedition to the Pacific, during which he visited the west coast of Australia and discovered the island of New Britain. In 1703 he was back to buccaneering again. On this occasion one member of his crew, Alexander Selkirk, made himself so unpopular that Dampier abandoned him on the remote islands of Juan Fernández, 483 km (300 miles) off the coast of Chile.

Selkirk survived on the island for four years. After his rescue, he returned to Britain. The author Daniel Defoe heard his accounts of his adventures and used them to form the basis of his novel *Robinson Crusoe*, which was published in 1719 and which has been popular ever since!

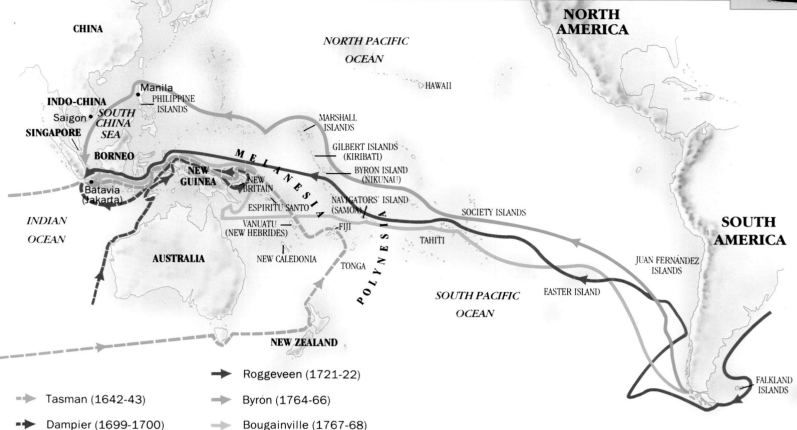

NORTH
AMERICA

NORTH PACIFIC
OCEAN

HAWAII

CHINA

INDO-CHINA
SINGAPORE
Saigon
SOUTH
CHINA
SEA
BORNEO
Batavia
(Jakarta)

Manila
PHILIPPINE
ISLANDS

MARSHALL
ISLANDS

GILBERT ISLANDS
(KIRIBATI)

BYRON ISLAND
(NIKUNAU)

NAVIGATORS' ISLAND
(SAMOA)

SOCIETY ISLANDS

SOUTH
AMERICA

NEW
GUINEA
NEW
BRITAIN
ESPIRITU SANTO
VANUATU
(NEW HEBRIDES)
FIJI
TAHITI
NEW CALEDONIA
TONGA

JUAN FERNÁNDEZ
ISLANDS

EASTER ISLAND

INDIAN
OCEAN
AUSTRALIA

SOUTH PACIFIC
OCEAN

NEW ZEALAND

FALKLAND
ISLANDS

Roggeveen (1721-22)

Byron (1764-66)

Bougainville (1767-68)

Tasman (1642-43)

Dampier (1699-1700)

Above It was Cook who eventually brought systematic exploration to the South Pacific. It had been visited by a number of other explorers, but their varying accounts made it hard to find isolated islands a second time.

Right The geysers of New Zealand inspired the wonder of the early missionaries and settlers. The most famous are at Rotorua, but hot springs are scattered over some 13 000 sq km (5 000 sq miles) of North Island.

Empty promises

In about 1840 a rumour spread through Europe that the French intended to claim New Zealand for themselves. The British government, which had held back settlement on the islands for several decades, now felt obliged to act. A warship was dispatched with instructions to make a treaty with the Maoris.

The Treaty of Waitangi was duly signed in 1840. The Maoris gave up sovereignty of their lands to Britain, but in return they were to have 'full and exclusive possession of their lands and estates'. This did not please the British settlers who had arrived in the same year. They pressed ahead with their claims to land despite the Treaty, triggering off the Maori Wars, which lasted from 1843 to 1872.

Flower of French exploration

After the end of the Seven Years' War in Europe in 1763, naval ships were sent abroad on missions of scientific discovery. One, commanded by Count Louis Antoine de Bougainville, sailed on France's first circumnavigation in 1767–1769. He laid to rest the idea that Vanuatu was a part of *Terra Australis*. He is remembered in the name of a flower, the *bougainvillea*.

SECTION 7: THE FINAL FRONTIERS

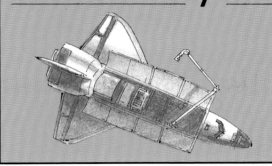

A century ago, much of the world had been explored. But there were still places — the North and South Poles, many mountain tops, the ocean depths — unvisited by humans. It took great courage and skill to reach these places and to confront the greatest challenge — space.

THE NORTH POLE

The first attempts to reach the North Pole were part of the long series of expeditions to find the Northeast and Northwest Passages (see pages 34-35 and 66-67). A persistent theory suggested that the North Pole might be surrounded by open sea, and a route to the East might lie across it. In 1827 a British naval officer, William Edward Parry (1790–1855), attempted to reach the Pole in boats hauled over the ice.

By the 1880s it was clear that the Pole lay in the middle of a permanent ice-cap. The race was on to see who could reach it using sledges and skis.

The winner was probably Robert Peary, an American, who claimed to have reached the Pole in 1909 with his black companion Matthew Henson and four Inuit (Eskimos). Peary was a coal engineer in the US Navy. In 1884 he was posted to Central America to work on a canal project in Nicaragua. But Peary preferred the chill of the polar regions to the heat of the sub-tropics. In his boyhood he had

Above The Arctic, one of the most inhospitable places in the world, is also one of the most underpopulated. Apart from a handful of research scientists and Inuit who have settled in various places there since 3000 BC, the area is virtually uninhabited.

Polar pioneer

In 1888, when he led an expedition across the Greenland ice sheet, Fridtjof Nansen (1861–1930) developed a sledge based on the *komatik*, the traditional Eskimo sledge.

To prove the theory that the icepack drifted eastwards from Siberia to the North Atlantic, Nansen commissioned the *Fram*, a ship strong enough to withstand the ice. He sailed north of Siberia where it became icebound. For three years it drifted westwards while the crew carried out detailed research.

Its path did not cross the Pole as Nansen had hoped, so he and a colleague left the ship and travelled over the ice with dog-drawn sledges and kayaks. They came within 402 km (250 miles) of the Pole — the farthest north anyone had been.

read about the adventures of Elisha Kent Kane, America's first polar hero. When he was posted back to the United States, polar exploration became his main interest, and in 1886 he made his first journey to Greenland.

Another American, Frederick Cook, created some bitterness when he claimed to have reached the Pole the year before. It was not until 1968 that the American Ralph Plaisted, using snow scooters, became the first person definitely to reach the North Pole by an overland route.

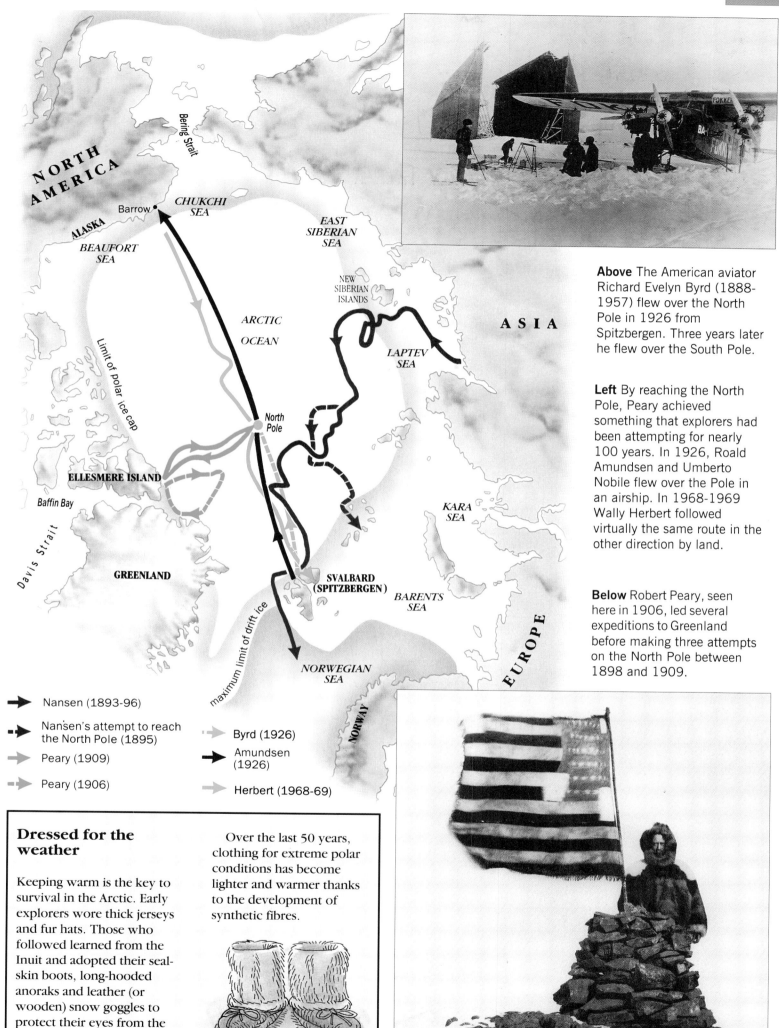

Above The American aviator Richard Evelyn Byrd (1888-1957) flew over the North Pole in 1926 from Spitzbergen. Three years later he flew over the South Pole.

Left By reaching the North Pole, Peary achieved something that explorers had been attempting for nearly 100 years. In 1926, Roald Amundsen and Umberto Nobile flew over the Pole in an airship. In 1968-1969 Wally Herbert followed virtually the same route in the other direction by land.

Below Robert Peary, seen here in 1906, led several expeditions to Greenland before making three attempts on the North Pole between 1898 and 1909.

➡ Nansen (1893-96)

➡ Nansen's attempt to reach the North Pole (1895)

➡ Peary (1909)

➡ Peary (1906)

➡ Byrd (1926)

➡ Amundsen (1926)

➡ Herbert (1968-69)

Dressed for the weather

Keeping warm is the key to survival in the Arctic. Early explorers wore thick jerseys and fur hats. Those who followed learned from the Inuit and adopted their seal-skin boots, long-hooded anoraks and leather (or wooden) snow goggles to protect their eyes from the fierce glare of the snow.

Over the last 50 years, clothing for extreme polar conditions has become lighter and warmer thanks to the development of synthetic fibres.

ANTARCTICA

The race for the South Pole began after Peary announced that he had reached the North Pole (see pages 80–81). Until then, various 19th-century explorers had reached the edges of Antarctica, and at the beginning of the 20th century they began to push into the interior of the continent.

Expeditions were mounted by Germans, Norwegians, Swedes, British, French, Japanese and Australians, mostly using ships with reinforced hulls to reach the base camps from which they made overland journeys. Among them was Robert Falcon Scott (1868–1912) who made two Antarctic journeys from 1901 to 1912.

The race was won by Roald Amundsen (1872–1928), an experienced Norwegian explorer. He reached the Pole on December 14, 1911, beating Scott's British team by just one month.

Today, about 30 research stations continue the work of these explorers studying the Antarctic's geology, climate and fauna. Travel has become easier with the use of motorized snow vehicles and light aircraft: powerful 'sno-cats' were used on Vivian Fuch's Trans-Antarctic expedition of 1957–1958.

Above Unlike the Arctic the Antarctic, a continent, is made of land covered with a deep layer of ice.

Right Ernest Shackleton (1874-1922) was one of the great Antarctic explorers. During his 1907-1909 expedition he came within 160 km (100 miles) of the Pole. He failed in his 1914-1917 expedition. In 1921 he set out on a third expedition but died in South Georgia a few months later.

Into the unknown

After Cook's second voyage during which he sailed right round the Antarctic (see pages 74-75), seal-hunters sailed to the remote islands bordering the Antarctic. Few, however, ventured further south.

Nonetheless, a growing scientific interest in the south polar region brought a series of navigators who began to chart its fringes. A Russian, Captain Fabian Gottlieb Bellingshausen, extended Cook's work by sailing around Antarctica in 1819-1821 and was probably the first to sight the Antarctic landmass. The British seal-hunter, Captain James Weddell, charted the area around the Antarctic Peninsula in 1823.

Captain James Clark Ross (left) was the most experienced polar explorer of his day. He had been on several Arctic expeditions before leading the British navy's first major Antarctic expeditions in 1839-1843. He discovered the sea and ice-shelf now named after him.

Believing that the work involved in pulling a sledge encouraged a sense of team spirit, his men (below) did not use dogs. This reluctance to use dogs had a decisive effect on the result of the final race for the South Pole. Captain Scott's team used ponies to pull their sledges. Too late, they realized that this was a mistake and shot the beasts before starting to haul the sledges themselves. Amundsen, who got to the Pole first, used dogs.

Above South Georgia. In 1914, after his ship, the *Endeavour*, was crushed by ice, Shackleton made a heroic 1 290-km (800-mile) journey in a small, open boat to this island.

'I am just going outside . . .'

In October 1911, Captain Scott set out from his base camp with four companions: Lawrence Oates, Edward Wilson, Edgar Evans and Henry Bowers. After an exhausting journey they reached the South Pole on January 17, 1912, but when they saw the tracks of Amundsen's team and the paw marks of his dogs, they realized they had been beaten to it.

Depressed, hungry and suffering from scurvy, they began the long journey home. Evans died. Then, Oates became ill and, knowing he was holding the rest up, he left the tent one night saying, 'I am just going outside and may be some time.' He walked to his death. Within a few weeks the others had also perished. Their frozen bodies, photographs and journals were found by a search party eight months later.

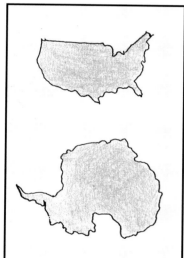

A vast wasteland

At 14 000 000 sq km (5 400 000 sq miles), Antarctica is larger than the entire United States of America. In winter, this area is extended by pack ice which forms when the sea water around the continent freezes. In several places flat areas of ice, called ice shelves, occupy the inner parts of the bays throughout the year.

Only in some parts of the Antarctic Peninsula are there areas where the land is exposed. The rest is permanently covered in ice.

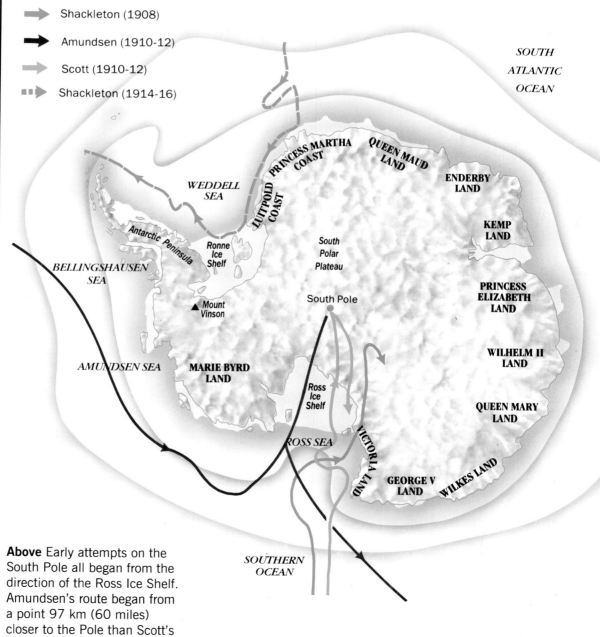

→ Shackleton (1908)
→ Amundsen (1910-12)
→ Scott (1910-12)
▪▪▶ Shackleton (1914-16)

SOUTH ATLANTIC OCEAN

PRINCESS MARTHA COAST
QUEEN MAUD LAND
ENDERBY LAND
LUITPOLD COAST
WEDDELL SEA
KEMP LAND
Antarctic Peninsula
Ronne Ice Shelf
South Polar Plateau
PRINCESS ELIZABETH LAND
BELLINGSHAUSEN SEA
▲ Mount Vinson
South Pole
WILHELM II LAND
AMUNDSEN SEA
MARIE BYRD LAND
Ross Ice Shelf
QUEEN MARY LAND
ROSS SEA
VICTORIA LAND
GEORGE V LAND
WILKES LAND
SOUTHERN OCEAN

Above Early attempts on the South Pole all began from the direction of the Ross Ice Shelf. Amundsen's route began from a point 97 km (60 miles) closer to the Pole than Scott's base camp.

Left Floodlighting shows up the unearthly beauty of a cave 500 m (1 640 ft) below the surface in France.

Right The world's highest peak, Mount Everest in the Himalayas. On May 29, 1953, Hillary and Tenzing set out from their camp to climb the final hundred or so feet. Five gruelling hours later, Everest had been conquered.

Below Mountain climbers not only have to scale sheer faces of rock, but they may also have to cross fields of melting ice and glaciers.

MOUNTAINS AND CAVES

The father of modern mountain-climbing was a Frenchman, Horace de Saussure (1740-1799). Before his time, only a few people had taken much interest in mountaineering. Saussure, a keen climber himself, offered a prize to the first person to climb Mont Blanc. It was over 20 years before it was claimed, by Michel Paccard, in 1786. By the late 19th century, mountain-climbing had become a popular pursuit, and climbers were using increasingly sophisticated equipment to reach ever-higher peaks. Today, all the highest mountains of the world have been scaled, but numerous peaks and mountain faces still present new challenges for climbers, as does the choice of methods used.

It was a Frenchman, too, who popularized speleology — the exploration and study of cave systems. The discovery of prehistoric remains in caves during the 18th century had stimulated interest in caves, but it was not until the late 19th century that Edward Alfred Martel championed and popularized speleology — at first in Europe. Today, speleologists travel all over the world to explore underground caves and cave systems.

On top of the world

Mount Everest, on the border between Nepal and China, was identified as the world's highest mountain in the 1850s.

There were at least eight failed attempts to conquer it before a carefully-planned British expedition led by John Hunt, set out in 1953.

With the help of Nepalese Sherpas as guides and porters, a series of camps was established on the mountain. The final stretch was climbed on May 29, 1953 by Edmund Hillary and Sherpa Tenzing.

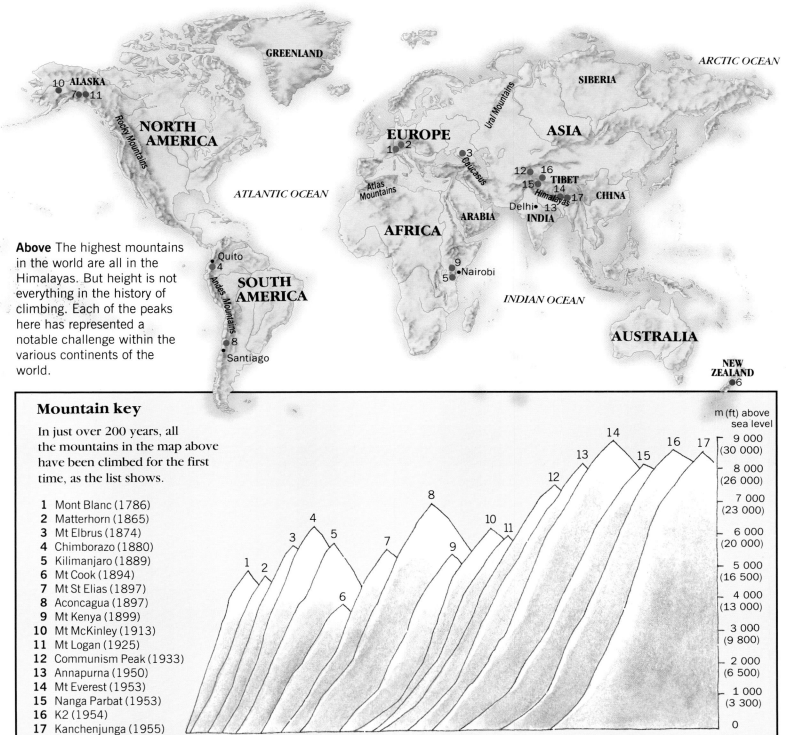

Above The highest mountains in the world are all in the Himalayas. But height is not everything in the history of climbing. Each of the peaks here has represented a notable challenge within the various continents of the world.

Mountain key

In just over 200 years, all the mountains in the map above have been climbed for the first time, as the list shows.

1 Mont Blanc (1786)
2 Matterhorn (1865)
3 Mt Elbrus (1874)
4 Chimborazo (1880)
5 Kilimanjaro (1889)
6 Mt Cook (1894)
7 Mt St Elias (1897)
8 Aconcagua (1897)
9 Mt Kenya (1899)
10 Mt McKinley (1913)
11 Mt Logan (1925)
12 Communism Peak (1933)
13 Annapurna (1950)
14 Mt Everest (1953)
15 Nanga Parbat (1953)
16 K2 (1954)
17 Kanchenjunga (1955)

m (ft) above
sea level

9 000
(30 000)

8 000
(26 000)

7 000
(23 000)

6 000
(20 000)

5 000
(16 500)

4 000
(13 000)

3 000
(9 800)

2 000
(6 500)

1 000
(3 300)

0

UNDERWATER EXPLORATION

Until the 20th century, most of what was known about the sea had been learnt from the surface. Surveyors on ships dropped lead weights on lines to measure the depth of the sea, and in the late 19th century scientists dredged up samples from the seabed and examined what they found. But they could not hope to have a complete picture until technological developments made it possible for them to see under water.

The first really efficient underwater breathing apparatus, the aqualung, was invented in the 1940s. Divers using aqualungs could descend up to 61 metres (200 ft). This opened up a whole new world for exploration. From the 1930s on, special diving machines were constructed to withstand the immense pressures of the ocean depths. The American naturalist William Beebe (1877–1962) created the bathysphere, a small spherical vessel which was lowered on a cable from a ship to a depth of 924 metres (3 032 ft) in 1934. Powered craft called submersibles, some operated by remote control, have since been developed and can explore the ocean floor to depths of 6 000 metres (19 680 ft).

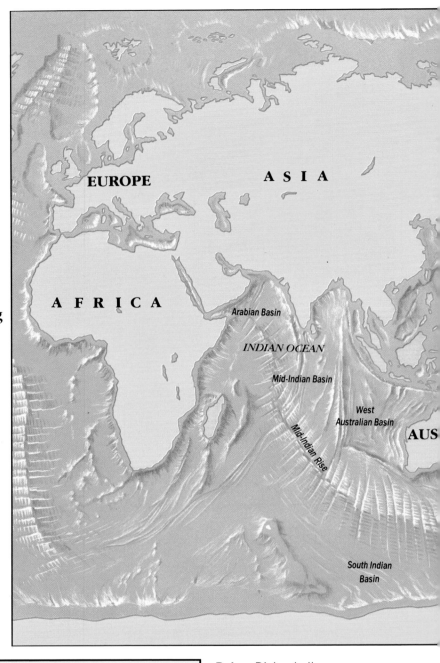

EUROPE

ASIA

AFRICA

Arabian Basin

INDIAN OCEAN

Mid-Indian Basin

West Australian Basin

Mid-Indian Rise

AUS

South Indian Basin

A challenging expedition

The first major study of the oceans was undertaken by the British ship HMS *Challenger* which circumnavigated the globe between 1872 and 1876. *Challenger* surveyed the complex topography beneath the waves for the companies laying submarine telegraph cables. The scientists on board also collected thousands of fish and plants.

Reports on the voyage took 25 years to complete and were published in 50 volumes, making an important contribution to the developing science of oceanography.

Below Diving bells were invented before diving suits and were used for such tasks as salvaging wrecks rather than for exploration. Once lowered into the water on a cable, they provided a bubble of air and dry, if cramped, working conditions for the operator. Edmund Halley's bell dates back to 1690. Fresh air was delivered to it in barrels.

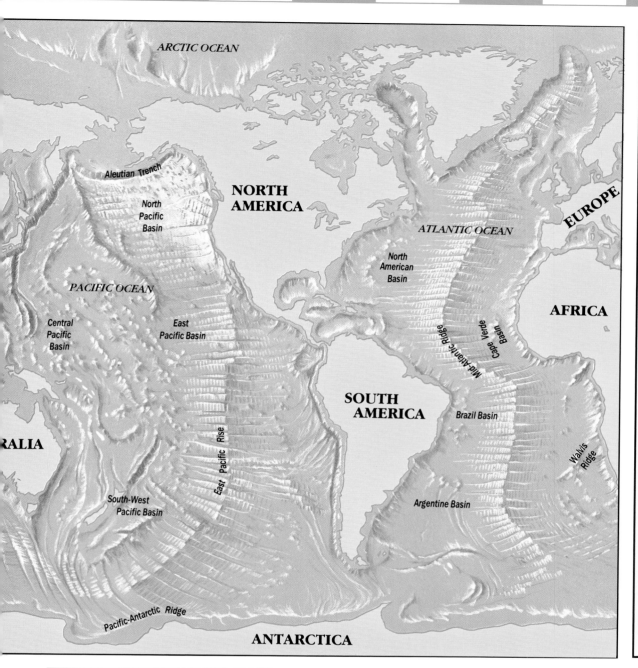

ARCTIC OCEAN

NORTH AMERICA

Aleutian Trench

North Pacific Basin

PACIFIC OCEAN

Central Pacific Basin

East Pacific Basin

ATLANTIC OCEAN

North American Basin

EUROPE

AFRICA

Mid-Atlantic Ridge

Cape Verde Basin

SOUTH AMERICA

Brazil Basin

Walvis Ridge

East Pacific Rise

South-West Pacific Basin

RALIA

Argentine Basin

Pacific-Antarctic Ridge

ANTARCTICA

Human gills

In 1825, William James developed the 'self-contained underwater breathing apparatus' which we now call SCUBA. Controlling the supply of air remained a problem until 1865 when Benoit Rouquayrol and Auguste Denayrouze made a breakthrough with the discovery of the regulating valve. This allowed air to pass only when the divers breathed in. In 1943, Jacques Cousteau attached a regulating valve to a tank of liquid compressed air to make the aqualung used by SCUBA divers today.

They came from under water

They may look like creatures from outer space, but they are, in fact, men wearing the diving suits of the 1840s and 1850s. The suits were made of thick waterproof canvas and the helmets of copper and glass. Air was supplied via tubes attached to a hand-pump on the surface.

The suits were worn by divers who needed to work underwater and could only be used in shallow water.

Above A physical map of the ocean floor shows its complex terrain. It occupies more than seven-tenths of the world's surface. Only a tiny portion of this has been fully explored.

Below The Swiss oceanographer Auguste Piccard (1884-1962) developed the bathyscape in the late 1940s. In 1960 a later version, the *Trieste,* was taken by his son, Jacques, to a depth of over 11 km (7 miles).

TRIESTE

US NAVY NEL ONR

Above During medieval times, various ideas about the heavens were proposed. After the Renaissance, astronomers began to assemble accurate pictures of our system.

INTO SPACE

People have always been fascinated by the heavens. The stars and planets have been the subject of intense study and speculation since ancient times and have played a central role in many religions. They have also played a vital part in the history of exploration.

However, the idea of exploring space remained totally impractical until the 20th century. German scientists developed a powerful rocket, the V-2, during the Second World War. Afterwards, they helped both the Soviets and the Americans develop rockets powerful enough to reach the speed necessary for space flight, a colossal 28 000 km/h (17 500 mph).

On October 4, 1957, the former Soviet Union launched *Sputnik 1*, the world's first artificial satellite — just 56 centimetres (22 in) in diameter. It orbited the Earth in just 92 minutes. One month later, the dog Laika, aboard *Sputnik 2*, became the first living creature in space.

The United States launched its first satellite, *Explorer 1*, on January 31, 1958. Just over a decade later, on July 20, 1969, two Americans landed on the Moon. They were the first of 12 Apollo astronauts to explore the lunar surface on foot in the greatest feat of exploration ever.

Left The American Robert Goddard, pictured on March 16, 1926, with his rocket, the first to use liquid fuel. He fired it successfully on a flight lasting 2.5 seconds.

Below The first stage in one of the greatest voyages of exploration. *Apollo 11*, with its three-man crew on board, blasts off from Cape Kennedy on July 16, 1969. Destination: the Moon.

Below The Earth as seen from *Apollo 11* after it had gone into lunar orbit. The few men and women who have seen the Earth from space have all remarked on how beautiful it is. A few hours after this picture was taken, two of the astronauts prepared to clamber into the lunar module that would land them on the Moon.

Above Yuri Gagarin, the first man in space, was ironically killed in a plane crash near Moscow, in 1968.

Below John Glenn being helped into his space suit just a few hours before he became the first American in space.

The race to the Moon

On April 12, 1961, Yuri Gagarin became the first man in space. He orbited the Earth once in *Vostok 1* and returned after 108 minutes. John Glenn became the first American astronaut on February 20, 1962.

The Soviets moved ahead when they landed an unmanned spacecraft, *Luna 9*, on the Moon in February 1966, a feat emulated by the Americans' *Surveyor 1* three months later.

The Americans pulled ahead with the launch of their *Apollo* missions.

Below The first woman in space was the Soviet, Valentina Tereshkova, in 1963.

We have the technology . . .

The two Saturn rockets that launched the Apollo astronauts. Below is the 68-m (223-ft) high *Saturn IB*, which launched Apollo astronauts on test flights into Earth orbit. On the left is the mighty *Saturn V* rocket, which launched the astronauts to the Moon. Standing 111 m (364 ft) high, it has a lift-off thrust of 3 500 tonnes — five times the power of the *Saturn IB*!

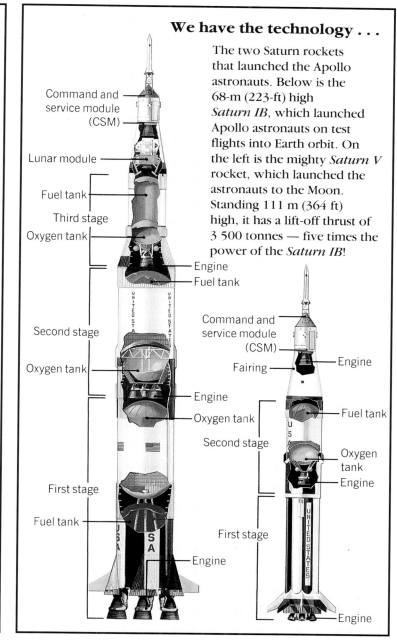

Command and service module (CSM) · Lunar module · Fuel tank · Third stage · Oxygen tank · Engine · Fuel tank · Second stage · Oxygen tank · Engine · Oxygen tank · First stage · Fuel tank · Engine · Command and service module (CSM) · Fairing · Engine · Fuel tank · Second stage · Oxygen tank · Engine · First stage · Engine

Below The *Apollo 11* lunar module, carrying Neil Armstrong and Edwin Aldrin, just after it has separated from the Apollo CSM mother ship. Michael Collins remains in the CSM as it continues in lunar orbit. Later it will rendezvous with the lunar module when that returns from the surface.

Below Edwin "Buzz" Aldrin climbs down the ladder of the *Apollo 11* lunar module to become the second man on the Moon. The photographer, Neil Armstrong, had become the first human being to set foot on the Moon a few minutes earlier. The historic date is July 20, 1969.

Right Mission complete, the *Apollo 11* lunar module prepares to dock in lunar orbit with the CSM.

Below Armstrong and Aldrin raise the Stars and Stripes as if to emphasize that the United States had clearly won the race to land men on the Moon.

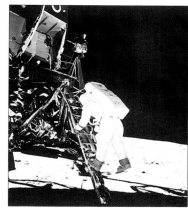

JOURNEYS TO THE PLANETS

By the time the last of the Apollo Moon landings took place, in December 1972, the next phase of space exploration was under way. It was the development of the space station, a large spacecraft in which astronauts could remain for long periods. The Soviet Union had launched its first space station, *Salyut 1*, in April 1971, but with little success.

In contrast, the first American space station, *Skylab* (launched May 1973), was a colossal success. Over a period of 10 months, three teams of astronauts lived on the station for longer and longer periods. The final crew stayed for 84 days, beating all space records. They proved that, properly equipped, human beings could survive in space for months.

In the 1980s Soviet cosmonauts repeatedly smashed the records, remaining in space for up to a year at a time in later *Salyuts*. Their current space station is called *Mir*.

After *Skylab*, the United States concentrated on developing the space shuttle. This is a re-usable craft which takes off like a rocket, but lands on an ordinary runway like a plane. The first shuttle flight into space, by the orbiter *Columbia*, took place on April 12, 1981. Since then, there have been over 50 shuttle missions.

While manned spacecraft have been exploring space near the Earth, unmanned space probes have been exploring outer space. They have flown into the depths of our solar system, and visited all the planets except Pluto.

Plans are now being considered for the next great leap in space exploration, manned expeditions to the planets. Perhaps the history of exploration is only just beginning.

Left In 1974 and 1975, *Mariner 10* flew past Mercury three times and sent back thousands of close-up images. Scientists put them together to produce this picture of the second smallest planet in the solar system. It is not much bigger than our Moon and like the Moon, it is pitted with craters.

Left A montage of images of Jupiter and its four large moons, sent back by *Voyager 1* in 1979 when it passed within 282 000 km (175 000 miles) of the giant planet. The picture shows the planet at the top and, going clockwise from it, the moons Callisto, Ganymede, Europa, and Io.

Below This montage of *Voyager 1* pictures, taken in 1980, shows Saturn and some of its moons. The probe discovered many new moons and several new rings. All the rings proved to be made up of narrow ringlets, caused by light reflected from rocks whizzing around the planet at high speed.

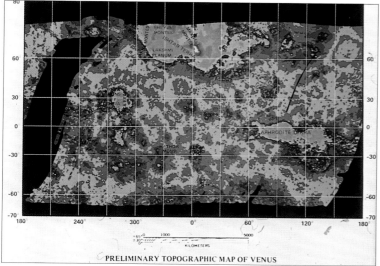

PRELIMINARY TOPOGRAPHIC MAP OF VENUS

Above *Pioneer Venus* went into orbit around Venus in 1978. It used radar to penetrate the thick clouds and produce images such as this.

Right With all engines blazing, the space shuttle orbiter *Atlantis* blasts off the launch pad at the Kennedy Space Center in Florida.

Left Mars, viewed by an approaching *Viking* space probe in 1976. Pictures taken by the two *Viking* landers reveal that Mars gets its colour from the red soil that covers most of its surface.

Now Voyager

In 1977, the United States launched two *Voyager* probes into the outer solar system. Both visited Jupiter and Saturn, and *Voyager 2* went on to Uranus and Neptune. *Voyager 2* reached Neptune in 1989. It arrived right on schedule after a journey of 12 years and 7 100 million km (4 400 million miles)!

The *Voyager* probes made many new discoveries about the planets they visited and sent back thousands of remarkable pictures. They discovered active volcanoes on Jupiter's moon Io; winds on Saturn blowing at 1 770 km/h (1 100 mph); chaotic landscapes on Uranus's moon Miranda; and liquid gas geysers on Neptune's moon Triton.

Left *Voyager 2* at Uranus in 1986. This picture montage shows the planet (background) and Miranda, one of its moons.

Right When *Voyager 2* flew past Neptune in 1989, it discovered that the planet is blue — due to the gases in its atmosphere.

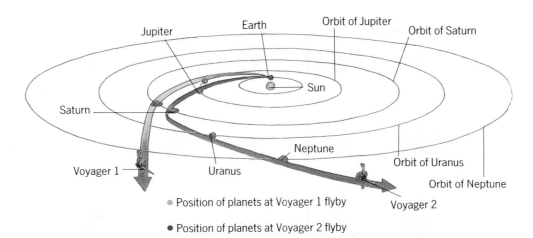

Jupiter · Earth · Orbit of Jupiter · Orbit of Saturn · Sun · Saturn · Neptune · Orbit of Uranus · Voyager 1 · Uranus · Orbit of Neptune · Voyager 2

• Position of planets at Voyager 1 flyby

• Position of planets at Voyager 2 flyby

TIME CHART

This time chart shows the landmarks of exploration (highlighted in green), and how they relate to the major events in world history. A glance at the time spans that separate the dates reveals how the pace of exploration accelerated rapidly during the 15th and 16th centuries and continued to increase from then on.

c. stands for circa, meaning about. It is used before dates which are approximate.

BC

c.9000	The beginnings of farming in Asia
c.8350	The foundation of Jericho, the first walled city
c.3000	The growth of the first great cities in Asia
	Early forms of writing develop
c.2600	The Great Pyramid built at Giza
c.2300	Harkhuf's expeditions up the River Nile
c.2000	The rise of Minoan civilization
c.1700	The beginnings of Chinese civilization
c.1500	The growth of the Hindu religion
1492	Queen Hatshepsut's expedition to the Land of Punt
c.1000	Town-building civilizations develop in Central America
814	The Phoenicians found Carthage
c.753	The foundation of Rome
c.600	Pharaoh Necho's expedition circumnavigates Africa
c.563	The birth of Buddha
334-323	Alexander the Great's expeditions in Asia
c.300	The early settlement of Polynesia
c.221	The Great Wall of China developed
146	The Greek world falls to the Romans
138	The voyage of Chang Chi'en to Central Asia
c.100	The development of the Silk Road across Asia

AD

c.30	The death of Jesus Christ
127-150	Ptolemy working at the Library of Alexandria
391	Christianity becomes the official religion of the Roman Empire
c.432	St Patrick brings Christianity to Ireland
476	Collapse of the Roman Empire
c.570-632	The life of the Prophet Muhammad
629-645	The voyage of Hsüan Tsang in Asia
711	The Muslim invasion of Spain
793	Viking raids on Europe begin
c.900	The collapse of the Mayan civilization
c.950	Maoris settle in New Zealand
1000	Leif Eriksson reaches North America
1096	The First Crusade
1206	The beginning of the Mongol conquest of Asia
1271-1295	Marco Polo's travels in Asia
c.1325	The rise of the Aztec Empire
1325-1354	Ibn Battuta's travels in Africa and Asia
1348	The Black Death devastates Europe
c.1350-1600	The Renaissance in Europe

1400

c.1400	The rise of the Inca Empire
1405-1433	Cheng Ho's naval expeditions, reaching Africa
1434	The beginnings of Portuguese exploration of West Africa under Henry the Navigator
1445	Gutenberg's Bible, Europe's first printed book, is produced
1453	Ottoman Turks capture Constantinople
1487	Pedro da Covilhā reaches India overland
	Bartolomeu Dias rounds the Cape of Good Hope
1492	Columbus reaches the Caribbean islands

1494	The Treaty of Tordesillas divides the New World between Portugal and Spain
1497	John Cabot reaches Newfoundland
1498	Vasco da Gama reaches India by sea
1499-1502	Amerigo Vespucci's expeditions to South America

1500

1500	Pedro Cabral reaches Brazil
1510	The first African slaves are taken to the Caribbean
1512	The Portuguese reach the Spice Islands
1513	Vasco de Balboa crosses Central America
	Juan Ponce de Léon reaches Florida
1517	Fernandez de Córdoba reaches Mexico
	Martin Luther initiates the Reformation
1519-1522	Ferdinand Magellan's expedition completes the first circumnavigation of the globe
1521	Hernán Cortés conquers the Aztecs
1532	Francisco Pizarro conquers the Incas
1534	Jacques Cartier sails up the St Lawrence River
1540-1542	Francisco Vásquez de Coronado and Garcia Lopez de Cárdenas explore south-west of North America
1542	Francisco de Orellana travels down the Amazon
1543	Juan Rodriguéz Cabrillo sails up the south-west coast of North America
1549	St Francis Xavier visits Japan
1571	The Spanish conquest of the Philippines
1577-1580	Francis Drake completes the second circumnavigation of the globe

1595 *The Dutch begin trading in South-East Asia*

1597 Willem Barents dies trying to find a Northeast Passage

1600

1606 Willem Jansz reaches Australia
1608 *The foundation of Quebec*
1609 *The invention of the telescope*
1611 The death of Henry Hudson
1620 *The Pilgrim Fathers land in New England*
1624 *New York founded by the Dutch*
1639 (-1853) *Japan is closed off to the world*
1642-1644 Abel Tasman's voyages around Australia and to New Zealand
1648 *The Taj Mahal is built in India*
1679-1682 Robert de La Salle travels down the Mississippi to the Gulf of Mexico

1700

1728 Vitus Bering sails through the Bering Strait
1759 *The conquest of Quebec by the British*
1768 James Bruce reaches the source of the Blue Nile
1768-1779 James Cook's three voyages in the Pacific and Southern Oceans
1776 *The American Declaration of Independence*
1786 Michel Paccard climbs Mont Blanc
1788 *The first settlements in Australia*
1789 *The French Revolution*
1792-1793 Alexander Mackenzie crosses North America
1795-1806 Mungo Park's expeditions in West Africa
1799-1804 Alexander von Humboldt's travels in South America

1800

1803 *United States buys Louisiana from France*
1804-1806 Meriwether Lewis and William Clark cross North America from St Louis to the west coast
1811 Thomas Manning reaches Lhasa
1815 *The defeat of Napoleon at Waterloo*
1825 *The opening of the first passenger railway, in northern England*
1828 René Caillié reaches Timbuktu
1831-1836 Charles Darwin's voyage on HMS *Beagle*
1837-1901 *The reign of Queen Victoria in Great Britain and Ireland*
1849-1855 Heinrich Barth crosses the Sahara
1853-1856 David Livingstone crosses Africa
1857-1858 *The Indian Mutiny*
1858 John Speke reaches Lake Victoria
1861 Robert Burke and William Wills die while trying to cross Australia
1861-1862 John Stuart successfully crosses Australia
1861-1865 *The American Civil War*
1864 Samuel and Florence Baker reach Lake Albert
1871 Henry Stanley finds Livingstone
1874 Stanley proves that Lake Victoria is the source of the Nile
1876 *The invention of the telephone*
1878-1879 Adolf Nordenkiöld sails the Northeast Passage
1895 Mary Kingsley's travels in the French Congo
The invention of radio

1900

1903 *The first successful powered flight, by the Wright Brothers*
1903-1906 Roald Amundsen sails the Northwest Passage
1909 Robert Peary reaches the North Pole
1911 Roald Amundsen reaches the South Pole
Machu Picchu discovered
1914-1918 *The First World War*
1917 *The Russian Revolution*
1924 Alexandra David-Néel reaches Lhasa
1930-1931 Bertram Thomas crosses the Empty Quarter of Arabia
1939-1945 *The Second World War*
1953 John Hunt's expedition conquers Mt Everest
1960 Jacques Piccard reaches the deepest part of the world's ocean floor in the bathyscape *Trieste*
1961 Yuri Gagarin becomes the first man in space
1969 Neil Armstrong and Edwin 'Buzz' Aldrin become the first men on the Moon
1989 *Voyager 2 reaches Neptune*

INDEX

ACKNOWLEDGEMENTS

Quarto would like to thank the following for providing photographs, and for granting permission to reproduce copyright material:

Aker/Turner: 61a; Janet and Colin Bord: 14a; Nick Buzzard: 62b, 68b; Cambridge University Library: 44b; Jean-Loup Charmet: 7cr, 9al, 10bl, 12b, 15ar, 20bl, 25bl, 27a, 32bl, 53ac, 87bl; Anthony R Dalton: 17ar; CM Dixon: 10ar, 12a, 13bl, 13br, 15al, 16bl, 16cr, 17br, 20br, 21cl, 23al, 23bl, 26a, 30c, 39c, 40b, 46bl, 63a, 66c, 70br; ET Archive: 6r, 7b, 8a, 8bl, 18a, 19b, 21br, 27b, 28c, 29b, 36a, 37c, 42b, 45c, 46br, 54a, 55a, 56c, 58bl, 62a, 63c, 65a, 66a, 67b, 71bl, 72b, 74b, 75br, 77a, 77b, 78b, 81a; The Fortean Picture Library: 7al, 33br, 78a; Leslie Garland Picture Library: 13a; The Hulton Picture Company: 84b; The Hutchison Library: 6l, 8br, 25br, 30a, 44a, 45b, 50b, 84c, 85a, John Dowman 55b, John Hatt 54br, Michael Macintyre 87cr, Bruce Wills 11c; Life File: Dr R Cannon 82a, Cliff Threadgold 23br; The Mansell Collection: 10br, 14b, 30b, 31a, 34c, 34b, 41b, 47br, 51a, 51b, 59b, 73bl, 86bl, 88a; NASA: 9ar, 88bl, 88br, 89cl, 89cr, 89bl, 89bc, 89br; National Maritime Museum: 35b, 58c; Peter Newark's Historical Pictures: 7ar, 24a, 48b, 49b, 52b, 53bl, 55c, 56b, 57a, 60b, 61b, 64b, 66b, 68al, 68c, 69bl, 69br, 74a, 81b, 82c, 82bl, 82br, 83ar, 86br, 87br; Panos Pictures: Alain Le Garsmeur 17c, 32ar, Ron Giling 43a, Neil Munns 42a, Bruce Paton 49b, David Reed 38c, 39b, Penny Tweedie 70bl; Quarto: 62c; Spacecharts: 88c, 89a, 89cl, 90a, 90bl, 90br, 91al, 91ar, 91cl, 91bl, 91br; Andrew Stewart: 40c, 41a, 50c; Trip: 47bl, 68ar, 80, 83al, Joan Batten 24bl, 52a, Colin J Conway 72a, Ian Fairweather 18br, Linda Jackson 32bl, Alexander Kuznetsov 34a, Bruce Low 71br, 72c, 79cr, Fiona Potter 64a, Richard Powers 58br, Helene Rogers 16br, 22b, 31b, 36b, 37a, 37b, 39a, 53ar, 56a, 57b, 75bl, Thelma Sanders 43b, 48a, 49a, Peter Saunders 26b, 42c, 46a, 63b, 71a, Joan Wakelin 73br, 76a, 76b, 79cl, Julia Waterlow 21bl; Michael Turner: 60a; Tony Waltham: 22a, 28a, 33a, 84a.

(a = above, b = bottom, c = centre, l = left, r = right)

Whilst every effort has been made to trace and acknowledge all copyright holders, we would like to apologize should any omissions have been made.